Runway's End

First there was 'Touchdown East L
'East Devon AirCrew & Airfields' (2000) and finally,
'Final Touchdown' (2005)

In '**RUNWAY'S END**' Grahame Holloway has recorded further stories from those who served as aircrew with the Armed Forces and whose service careers were not covered in the earlier books. All are members of either the East Devon or Taunton & Tiverton Aircrew Associations and now live in the West Country. Early chapters covering the RAF presence in East and South Devon have been updated with new entries added covering the former airfields at Winkleigh and Chivenor in Devon and Merryfield and Weston Zoyland in West Somerset. Other Associations with a close affinity to the Aircrew Association are also included.

The photograph on the front cover is of the now deserted runway at former RAF Upottery in East Devon which played a prominent role on D-day, being the take-off point for over a thousand US paratroops.

Published by

'BREVET 2000'

The Publishing Section
of the
East Devon Aircrew Association.

C/o The RAFA Club, Imperial Road,
Exmouth, EX8 1DB

Printed by:
imprint digital
Upton Pyne, Exeter, EX5 5HY
www.imprintdigital.net

First Published 2011

Copyright © East Devon Aircrew Association

ISBN 978-0-9539015-3-1

Contents

Subject	Page
Dedication and Acknowledgements	4
Introduction	5 - 6
About the Author	7
The Aircrew Association	8 – 10
The Initial Training of Aircrew	11
Devon hotels Requisitioned	12 – 19
Aircrew Casualties	20
RAF Hospital, Torquay. (aka The Palace Hotel)	21 – 27
The First & Last RAF aircraft based in Devon	28
RAF Airfields in Devon & West Somerset	29 - 87
(Listed alphabetically)	
Introduction to 'Those who Served'	88
Members' service and personal recollections	89 - 205
(Names listed in alphabetic order)	
'After the Final Landing'	206
The AirCrew Association Archive Trust	207 - 211
The Royal Air Forces Association	212 - 213
The Aircrew Memorial on Plymouth Hoe	214 - 215
The South West Airfields Heritage Trust	216 - 217
Glossary	218

DEDICATION

This book is dedicated to all aircrew, whether still flying or having reached the 'runway's end' for the last time, and who have served in the armed forces of Her Majesty or Her Allies and have been awarded an approved brevet recognising their training to operate as a skilled member of the aircrew fraternity.

ACKNOWLEDGEMENT

Firstly the East Devon Aircrew Association acknowledges with grateful thanks all those members who, reluctantly in some cases, have provided the material to make this book possible.

Thanks also go to the many others who, behind the scenes, provided photographs and encouragement and, in particular, to David Laskey without whose computer skills the task would have been much harder. Lastly, but not least, thanks goes to 'Dick' Ward for his painstaking proof reading of the original manuscript.

All profits arising from the sale of this book will be distributed by the Committee of the East Devon Aircrew Association in furtherance of the Association's aims and such charities as may be supported by it.

INTRODUCTION

When, with the help of a local newspaper group, the East Devon Branch of the Aircrew Association produced their first book, 'Touchdown East Devon' in 1997, they had no idea how successful it would become and the meagre print run was quickly exhausted. Three years later with new members joining the branch, there was enough material for a second book and so, in 2000, 'East Devon Aircrew & Airfields' was published, this time by the Branch itself. However, once again, caution prevailed and within twelve months all books were sold. However, there is nothing like success breeding success and in 2005 *Grahame Holloway,* who was then Branch Chairman, completed the last of a trilogy which was entitled 'Final Touchdown'. With the advancing years of the majority of members it was intended that this would be the last. The approach was bolder with members from the neighbouring Torbay branch contributing their reminiscences and the number of airfields covered expanded to include the whole of South Devon and Dartmoor fringe.

Today, there are still frequent enquiries about the characters who contributed to the earlier books. Sadly 60% of those who contributed the first have now passed on so, too, have 40% who contributed to the second. Many of the survivors are now in their ninth decade, some enjoying better health than others. On the plus side the East Devon Aircrew Association is still attracting new members, albeit at a much slower pace than in the past. Today, together with colleagues from the neighbouring *Taunton & Tiverton Association,* as well as reminiscences of WWII they bring stories of the 'Cold War' and conflicts from the Falklands to Afghanistan. **"Runway's End'** covers their experiences as military aircrew.

However for new readers we are also re-writing the early chapters on the RAF's presence in Devon but expanding previous coverage to Mid and North Devon with the inclusion of the airfields at RAF Winkleigh and RAF Chivenor. Together with reminiscences from members of the Taunton & Tiverton Aircrew Association, also included are details of two former RAF stations in West Somerset, namely Merryfield and Weston Zoyland.

However no record of the RAF in Devon would be complete without some mention of the Associations which exist to preserve our aircrew heritage or to help those former airmen sadly now in need. In addition to once more covering the history behind the Allied Aircrew Memorial on Plymouth Hoe, this time the excellent work undertaken by the Aircrew Archive Trust, the Royal Air Forces Association and the South West Airfields Heritage Trust has been included for the first time.

Having written a number of 'aircrew obituaries' for a local paper, the editor once said to Grahame Holloway, "What a shame we never hear of these stories whilst they are still alive and have to wait until they are dead to learn about them," a remark which led to the writing of the earlier trilogy. In **'Runway's End'** the author pursues the original aims.

Firstly, and most important, is the recording of the members' recollections of life as a member of military aircrew. As with our previous books, copies of 'Runway's End' will be lodged with the Imperial War Museum, The Centre for WWII Studies and the Aircrew Archive Trust for research by future scholars and historians. The second aim is to provide a modest profit so that the aims of the Aircrew Association can continue with the support of local aircrew veterans and the charities to which they, in turn, subscribe.

 ## The Author

As you will discover, this work contains recollections and reminiscences from many sources. These have been researched over the past fourteen years by **Grahame Holloway** to provide the fourth in a series of books recounting the service life of local aircrew.

A former RAF National Service pilot, Grahame trained in Canada on T-6's in the early 1950's. Returning to the UK, he converted onto the de Havilland Vampire before seeing further service with the RAFVR and R.Aux.AF. Later, during the height of the 'Cold War' and whilst pursuing a career in the Police Service, he was one of only a handful of police officers trained for specialist flying duties should a nuclear attack be made on Britain. He retired in 1986 as a Superintendent.

Post retirement, he served with the Royal Observer Corps until its disbandment in September 1991. As a Group Officer his RAF connections occasionally saw him flying on sorties with Nimrods of No. 42 Squadron, RAF St. Mawgan, and on Hercules training flights from RAF Lyneham. A former Chairman, he is currently PRO and Asst. Secretary of the East Devon Aircrew Association. His hobbies include travel and writing. As well as the author of the three previous books in this series, his other works include *"Copper's Devon"* and *"Battles, Bullets & Mayhem"*.

The Aircrew Association

"The Aircrew Association was founded on the 8th September 1977 to foster comradeship amongst aircrew who had been awarded a military flying badge. Membership is open to those who are serving or have served as military aircrew in the armed forces of those nations allied to the United Kingdom and Commonwealth. By 2010 more than 25,000 military aircrew had joined and in its formative years it attracted members who had served during the Second World War. In recent years the ACA has attracted aircrew from the Cold War era and from those currently serving as military aircrew"

The above is the inscription on the Aircrew Memorial at the National Memorial Arboretum at Alrewas in Staffordshire. Only those who have experienced the thrill of flight can really understand the strong bond which exists between those who have not only flown but also known the comradeship of service life. It is a bond further strengthened by their intimate knowledge of an environment unknown to many ... the sky! Majestic and without boundaries yet it conceals many dangers. For military aircrew this may be threats from an enemy, whilst for others their fight was against the elements. It is not surprising, therefore, that this special bond resulted in the formation of the Aircrew Association whose membership is uniquely limited to those who have served as aircrew in the Armed Forces of Her Majesty, or Her Allies, and have been awarded a 'recognised flying badge'. Drawn from the Royal Air Force, the Royal Navy and Army Air Corps, today the veteran air gunners, bomb aimers, flight engineers and wireless operators of WWII are joined not only by pilots and navigators but by weapon systems and air electronics operators, helicopter crewmen and air loadmasters of the modern age.

Theirs is a proud heritage and in its heyday the Association fostered over a hundred branches in Britain with others spread throughout the Commonwealth and the United States. Others would be found in ex-pat conclaves such as Cyprus and parts of Spain. All were linked by the Association's quarterly Magazine, *'Intercom'*. *'The Aircrew Association Charitable Fund'*, a registered charity, exists to provide speedy 'FIRST AID' to members in need.

In addition, the *'Aircrew Association Archive Trust'* recognises the importance of preserving aircrew archives and memorabilia for future generations to study and enjoy. The Trust's aim is to preserve such items and it now has a permanent home and display at the Yorkshire Air Museum, a county once the home of many bomber squadrons during WWII.

Sadly, the past thirty years have seen many cut-backs within our armed forces. Some have been due to economic pressures whilst others because of changing requirements. Today one RAF Tornado with a crew of two has the capacity to inflict more collateral damage than a whole squadron of WWII Lancaster bombers with almost a hundred men. Invariably the pool of aircrew has been shrinking year by year. Coupled with this is the fact that current members of the Association are becoming increasingly older. WWII veterans are now in their late 80's or even older and many branches are beginning to close as they are unable to form active committees. The same is also being experienced at national level, a problem which led to the Executive Council deciding that with effect from the end of 2011 it would no longer function as an international Association but the future would be left in the hands of individual branches with continuity provided by The Aircrew Association Archive Trust.

Fortunately, the East Devon Aircrew Association is one of the country's strongest and enjoys an active committee comprising almost exclusively post-war aircrew. It was founded in 1991 by Don Francis, a former navigator who flew Mosquitoes with a 'special duties' squadron during the war and later became the Chief Draughtsman for the De Havilland Blue Streak project.

Initially known as the Exmouth & District Branch its growth led to a change of name to 'East Devon' to also include the City of Exeter. However, whilst most of its current membership resides in the area it is by no means exclusive. In fact it draws membership from a much wider area having absorbed the former Plymouth branch's membership when it closed in 2005. It also has members who commute from neighbouring Somerset and from North and West Devon. With such expanding horizons even the branch's current title may need a further change in the future.

Meetings are held at the RAFA Club, Imperial Road, Exmouth, at 7.30 pm on the 2nd Tuesday of each month when there is a speaker with topics differing widely from month to month. There is also a full social programme which includes monthly pub lunches in both the East Devon and Plymouth areas, buffets, and visits to interesting venues and events. All members are kept aware of events by way of EDACA NEWS, a monthly newsletter.

All serving or former members of aircrew from the armed forces will be made more than welcome at any of their events.

The INITIAL TRAINING of AIRCREW

This book is about aircrew, their airfields, aircraft and reminiscences of service life. However, long before they set foot inside an aircraft they have to go through a rigorous selection process followed by a period of ground training.

During WWII Torquay provided facilities for the initial training of many thousands of potential aircrew and the rare photograph produced below shows two such recruits walking along The Stand, Torquay, in an off-duty moment.

The airman on the left is Jack Atkinson of Sampford Peverel, near Tiverton, who attended the ITW at The Beacon Hotel in 1941. He later qualified as a pilot and a long career followed with aircraft flown during WWII including the Hurricane. Tomahawk and Mustang and, post war, the Vampire and Meteor jet fighters. He eventually retired in 1963 as a Squadron Leader.

The role played by a number of Torbay's hotels will be explored in the following pages.

Devon Hotels - Requisitioned

The scale of conflict during WWII was immense and all three of our armed forces needed a constant supply of manpower to ensure sufficient resources to pursue the course of victory and to replace the inevitable casualties of battle.

Bomber Command deaths alone exceeded over 55,000 with thousands more injured and the influx of volunteers to enlist in the RAF as aircrew was at times overwhelming which, in itself, provided a major problem. Put simply, the RAF did not have the capacity to train high numbers of new recruits. Operational airfields were fully committed to their principle task of fighting the war in the air with their fighter or bomber aircraft on constant readiness. In turn they, too, were potential enemy targets and indeed many sustained serious damage and suffered human casualties from Luftwaffe attacks. In other words, they were completely unsuitable for recruit training.

Flying Training Schools did exist but were geared to a pre-war intake and not the mass influx now being experienced. Being based at airfields these, too, would have been vulnerable to enemy attack. However there was another solution, namely, to requisition accommodation suitable for initial training of aircrew. In practice this meant large hotels situated in resort areas which were more remote from normal target areas. Here hotels at Torquay and Paignton were to make a major contribution and also to a lesser extent did hotels at Sidmouth. Requisitioned by the RAF these hotels performed two roles. Firstly, recruits would arrive at Aircrew Reception Centres (ACRC's) to be kitted out, inoculated etc. and then passed to the second stage, known as 'Initial Training Wings' (ITW). Each was allocated an identifying number e.g. No.2 ITW Torquay and here recruits would complete the first stage of their aircrew training. All would face the ritual of parade ground drill, known in the services as 'square bashing' and embarking on a strenuous programme of physical fitness. This was followed by basic classroom instruction in a variety of subjects of relevance to their later postings.

Of all the towns in the UK where requisition was at its highest, arguably Torbay's combination of Torquay and Paignton came close to topping the list. A few still function today as hotels within the resort. Examples include: the Sefton Hotel on Babbacombe Downs Road which, at various times, was used as both an ACRC and ITW.

One former bomber pilot, John Morgan of Sidmouth, recalls his second day there in 1940. He says he had been issued with only part of his uniform and had gone down the road dressed in RAF trousers, held up by standard issue white webbing belt, a civilian shirt and no hat. Suddenly a large saloon car pulled up beside him and a young officer jumped out. "Why didn't you salute the flag", he demanded. "What flag"? John asked. The small pennant on the front of the car was pointed out to him and he was told that it denoted an Air Commodore was on board. With that the rear door opened and John was beckoned over by the very senior officer whom it transpired was doing an inspection tour of the area's training facilities. Answering his questions John explained it was only his second day and that was all the uniform he had. Upon this he was ordered to 'double back' to the hotel. "What does 'double' mean", John innocently asked. "It means run you bloody fool, run", came the terse reply. Incidentally, John's flying career came to an abrupt end on the 12th August 1941. He was briefed for his first 'op', a raid on Berlin and piloted his aircraft to within sight of the city when it was hit my enemy fire and burst into flames. With a full bomb load on board he and his crew wasted no time in baling out. Injured in the process, he was taken prisoner of war. He was only nineteen.

As well as an ACRC the **Sefton Hotel** also became No.1 ITW and one person who undertook his initial training there was the late Arthur McCartney who later became the Deputy Chief Constable of the former Devon Constabulary. He once recounted, *"My unit from ACRC arrived late in the year. We swam or paddled in the sea on Christmas Day 1941. We were housed in the **Sefton Hotel** on Babbacombe Cliff Road and ate in a hotel, the name of which I have been unable to recall but was in the Cary Park district. At the top of the road through the village was the Babbacombe Garage where we were instructed in navigation the basement. Our course was completed early in 1942 and I remember how we formed up and marched from the **Sefton Hotel** to Torre Railway Station. To me it was reminiscent of films I had seen at the cinema with troops marching off to war in the Great War. We sang 'It's a Long Way to Tipperary' and 'Roll me Over' and such but we were only going to the Elementary Navigation School in Eastbourne!"* Then he added, *"I also remember a very attractive young lady who worked in a cake shop along the main road. She was certainly an asset to the owner; we were always popping in there for cakes and buns! I'm sure eventually she must have married someone who became aircrew and I often wonder what happened to her. So many husbands were killed, I hope she was lucky."*

Arthur went on to become one of Bomber Command's most experienced Bomb Aimers, participating in thirteen of the sixteen major raids on Berlin and is thought to be the only Air Bomber' to be twice awarded the DFC. Sadly Arthur passed away on his 89th birthday on the 3rd March 2008

By co-incidence another former senior officer of the local Constabulary also undertook basic training in Torquay. He was Alf Wallen who says *"I was at No.13 ITW which was based in Torquay's **Grand Hotel**. Our course director was Flying Officer Tom Goddard, an excellent cricketer who played for Gloucestershire and was an England spin bowler. Most mornings it was*

PT behind Torquay railway station followed by marching up and down Torquay sea front at 140 paces a minute. Nearly all our course work was done in the **Grand Hotel** but occasionally we would parade on the Green about three hundred yards from the **Grand** and take down morse code messages sent by Aldis Lamp from a bedroom at the **Belgrave Hotel.**

Alf was later commissioned and became a navigator with No.514 Squadron flying Lancasters. Their targets included industrial sites on the Ruhr and although their aircraft was damaged a few times he says he survived uninjured. Alf now lives in retirement at Budleigh Salterton.

The Setton (above left) and The Grand (above right) were two of Torquay's hotels requisitioned by the RAF for the initial training of aircrew.

Ninety-year old Jack Atkinson of Sampford Peverell, who featured on the introductory page, recalls his initial training at No. 2 ITW between April and June 1941. He says much of the experience is a now a blur. However he then added:

"I was stationed in a small hotel on the Harbour front which I believe was called '**The Beacon'**. I remember the PTI's marching our entry up and down by the harbour and also there was a running track on Daddy Hole Plain which is also where we were given Aldis lamp instruction. However I

15

suppose my main recollection is of the pubs and an early visit one morning by a Heinkel 111 which caused us some consternation when it opened machine gun fire on us before dropping its bombs nearby. Thankfully, none of us were hurt but it was a close call. It's funny to look back now but a few months later we were doing the same thing."

Another Torbay seafront hotel which was commandeered by the RAF was The **Tembani at** Paignton although it has since been converted. Ninety year old former pilot John Legg of Budleigh Salterton recalls being there between the 24th August and 11th October 1940 and how they were marched everywhere singing such songs as 'I've got sixpence' and 'Nellie Dean', renderings which he says were much appreciated by the locals! He says they could not afford much 'night-life' on two shillings (20p) a day.

One interesting moment he recalls was being marched to the grassy area above the Babbacombe Cliff to be addressed by the 'Father of the RAF' Lord Trenchard who always carried a walking stick. However, his talk was interrupted by an air-raid warning just as a German Ju-88 flew overhead from inland and headed out to sea with Lord Trenchard waving his stick. On another occasion John was on guard duty when, early in the morning, the corporal in charge came out and gave him five rounds of .303 ammunition, announcing there was believed to be an invasion further down the coast to the West. He says he never did find out what led to the scare.

Don Francis recalls his ITW days at yet another Torquay hotel, **The Templestowe** situated in Tor Church Road. He had been working in the aircraft industry since leaving school and joined the Royal Auxiliary Air Force as an aero-engine fitter in 1937, volunteering for full-time service in February 1939. When war was declared he was restricted from volunteering for aircrew but when the opportunity arose in the summer of 1942 he wasted no time in doing so and was selected for navigator training.

He says, *"I arrived at the Templestowe in August 1942 as an LAC (Leading Aircraftsman) with one Good Conduct Badge. Being a visible indication of service - three years of undetected crime - it worried the newly appointed corporal PTI's who expected me to be an 'awkward type'. However, the threat, constant through aircrew training, of being failed 'LMF' (Lack of Moral Fibre) kept my awkwardness under control. I even helped one of the junior officers by giving talks on Air Force Law and procedure! I was also put in charge of the squad and responsible for marching them to lectures. PT was a regular feature. This mostly comprised of a run to Cockington where we took refreshment, at our own expense, in the Drum Inn where, incidentally, the NCO in charge of us always seemed to have a 'freebie'. Then we would hang around until it was time to return, a journey which would usually find us running into the sea dressed in our shorts and singlets. Dinghy drill was a not to be forgotten experience with us lining up to jump off the harbour wall into the sea which, when the tide was out, could be a drop of up to fourteen feet. Then we would swim to a one-man dinghy into which we would climb with difficulty. "*

Don qualified as a navigator and went on to fly thirty-five ops with a 'special duties' Mosquito squadron engaged on low level intruder missions. After the war he returned to a career in aviation and became De Havilland's Chief Draughtsman for their 'Blue Streak' missile project, before joining British Aerospace from which he retired in 1981. He is still a Member of the Royal Aeronautical Society.

As part of his 90th birthday celebrations, in July 2009 Don returned to the Templestowe Hotel on a nostalgic visit. Needless to say he was made very welcome by the staff on his arrival!

Above: Don, aged ninety, at the Templestowe

Other Torbay hotels used for the initial training of aircrew included The **Palm Court,** the home of No.5 ITW, **The Devonshire** and **Foxlands**. In fact it has been estimated that between 1939 and 1944 some 149,000 trainee aircrew passed through the Torbay hotels.

In Sidmouth the hotels provided accommodation for a different type of training. An 'Officer's Training School' was set up in the town between 1942-43, drawing students from aircrew officers who had undertaken their flying training abroad but had yet to join an operational squadron. A 'Battle Training Ground', with a commando' style assault course and a grenade range, was provided on Mutters Moor, a tract of open moor high above the town on the road to Otterton. Camouflage techniques were also taught, an essential subject bearing in mind the object of the course was to teach how to evade capture if shot down in hostile territory.

Today visitors to the town do not realise that the car park near the **Bedford Hotel** was once a drill square whilst aircrew were stationed in the hotel itself together with other hotels such as the **Knole, Belmont** and **Fortfield**. The officers' mess was in the **Riviera Hotel** and that for Sergeants in the

Torbay. The **Victoria Hotel** housed the medical section.

Very little vestiges of the assault course or grenade range remain on Mutters Moor but one reminder of those days has been preserved on the cliff top at the entrance to Connaught Gardens, only a short walk from the Victoria Hotel and on the way to Mutters Moor. This is a gun emplacement which is now embellished with a 'Blue Plaque' signifying it as part of the town's heritage.

Above left is the impressive Victoria Hotel. On the right, is the town's reminder of WWII, the gun emplacement in Connaught Gardens.

Local hotels were also commandeered in other locations and for other purposes. For instance, naval aircrew flying from Haldon were billeted in a Teignmouth hotel and similar local accommodation was found for the RAF Marine Unit at Exmouth.

AIRCREW CASUALTIES

The training of aircrew was expensive. Building new aircraft was relatively easy but replacing highly trained aircrew was not. The casualty rate for those who flew was high. Indeed by the time WWII ended Bomber Command alone had lost over 55,000 young men killed whilst many times that number were injured. In addition, such losses in percentage terms were just as high for those serving in Coastal Command and engaged in the relentless search for enemy U-boats. Neither were the pilots of Fighter Command immune.

For those who fortunately escaped death often a period of incapacity due to injury followed but during the height of the war it was essential they returned to operational flying as soon as possible.

Left: Kay Lawrence, nee Harte, one of the VADs at RAF Hospital, Torquay in 1942

Initial treatment for injuries sustained in battle was, wherever possible, carried out at hospitals closest to where they were landed. However, such were the strains upon their resources that it became essential for the wounded to be moved to other medical establishments for recuperation and any remedial surgery which may be needed later. A number of RAF Hospitals were established for this purpose, one being in Torquay.

RAF HOSPITAL, TORQUAY

As the result of a forward thinking policy concerning the necessity of returning injured aircrew to operational fitness as soon as possible, the **Palace Hotel** in Torquay was requisitioned as a RAF hospital as early as October 1939. Adaptations were quickly made within this luxury hotel, which pre-war had 5* status, to provide all the facilities necessary for the post-operative recuperation for those transferred from the main hospitals but, in addition, a fully equipped operating theatre was also installed to provide the follow-up surgery which, unfortunately, often became necessary. Interestingly, because of its luxurious facilities, it was designated for use by officer aircrew only! In practice, however, many of the operations undertaken were on the recruits injured whilst undergoing training at the local ITWs.

RAF Hospital, Torquay, as it appeared in 1941

It was as RAF Hospital, Torquay, that the Palace Hotel entered the annals of local history at around 1110 hours on the morning of Sunday, 25th October 1942. That was the hour when a flight of four Luftwaffe FW-190s took the town by surprise and administered a devastating blow. They flew back across the Channel to their base near Caen in Normandy leaving many dead and injured. Particularly badly hit was the RAF Hospital at the Palace where a direct hit had virtually demolished the east wing.

Above: Bomb damage at RAF Hospital, Torquay, after the raid on 25th October 1942.

A newspaper report dated the next day gave an account of the raid but, because of censorship, made no reference of the fact it was a RAF Hospital. The opening paragraph read as follows:

'Flying low along the coast yesterday morning four FW190's swerved over a South-West seaside town, dropping bombs and firing cannon before turning out to sea again, but not at least before one of them was seen leaving a trail of smoke. The leading plane dived to tree-top height to make a direct hit on a hospital. It is feared that casualties amongst both men and women are high.'

Their assumption that casualties were high was not wrong for reports indicated the hospital had its full complement of 203 beds. Fortunately many of the convalescing patients were out at the time or else the toll of twenty killed and over forty injured would have been very much higher. However, it is understood this later rose as some of the patients who were evacuated immediately after the raid succumbed to their injuries at their new locations. In fact one newspaper later reported the death toll as thirty-seven.

For an event which occurred nearly seventy years ago it is rare indeed to have an eye-witness still able to give a detailed account. Fortunately one exists and she is Kay Lawrence, nee Harte, who resides with her husband, Keith, in Exeter. Early in the war she was one of many women who volunteered for duty with the VAD (Voluntary Aid Detachment), a detachment of the Red Cross, and in 1942 she was serving at RAF Hospital, Torquay. Kay had been assisting the surgeon in the operating theatre when the bombs dropped. Her contemporary diary entry makes for poignant reading and she has given permission for it to be reproduced here.

"In the Theatre when we were bombed at 11.10 - one direct hit & one v. near miss - 19 killed, not all found - ghastly thing - rain fell all day - we evacuated patients injured (40) to sick quarters at the Torbay and ours to Wroughton - just a few of the ill ones. It was an amazing thing - no panic. Little Tinker-Bell was killed also G/C Whittle. W/C Burke, Luddington and many others. - we, all the VAD's, were sent to a nursing home for the night."

Then entries for the following days continue with that for Monday, 26th October: beginning: *"Hectic day disposing of patients - sick leave or Wroughton for most of them. More bits of bodies found - awful. .... "*

In speaking to Kay about the aftermath she explained:

"Our primary task was to evacuate all of our patients which we did with the utmost of speed, but to continue treatment at their new hospitals it was also necessary for their notes to follow them, and that was my job. I spent the next six days in what can best be described as rubble without windows trying to sort all the records out. Fortunately most survived and were forwarded on as required and then I, too, said goodbye to The Palace."

In fact, to this day Kay maintains that being in the theatre probably saved her life. There was no warning before they heard the first bomb fall, landing just away from the building itself. Nevertheless the blast made the building shake to such an extent that it dislodged the light above the operating table. Then, only moments later, the second bomb hit and virtually demolished the hospital's east wing. Had she not been in the Theatre Kay would have been in her office and undoubtedly either killed or seriously injured by the blast.

When the war ended in 1945 Kay was to marry one of the hospital's former patients. He was Keith Lawrence, a dashing young New Zealand Spitfire pilot who had been shot down over the Channel during the Battle of Britain. He was later to command his own squadron during the siege of Malta and was awarded the DFC. After the war he settled in Britain with Kay and, now in his nineties, is a member of the East Devon Aircrew Association.

For another perspective of life at the hospital through the eyes of a former in-patient we turn to Norman Conquer, a retired Wing Commander who now lives in Okehampton. The sole survivor when his Blenheim bomber crashed, he spent eight months in hospital before being sent to The Palace to convalesce. He gave the following account in 2005.

"What a splendid place to choose as an officers' convalescent home. For most of us our treatment began in the hotel gym immediately on arrival and we soon discovered that physiotherapy at the hotel was in the charge of Dan Maskell, of tennis fame. My room mate was a Canadian pilot who survived a crash but suffered arm and neck injuries, his tall neck-brace making him look like a 'giraffe' lady from Africa! With my leg in a full length plaster we were an odd couple! However despite our handicaps we soon discovered a bus stop only a hundred yards from the hotel and most convenient for daily forays into town although, unfortunately, my plaster would not allow me the luxury of sitting down for the journey. Needless to say we enjoyed the hospitality of the local pubs! Sadly there were always events to highlight the fact we were still very much at war. A few days after I left to return to duty the Palace was bombed by FW 190 intruders and several of the inmates killed. One really never knew what might be in store."

As to the raid itself, this was not altogether unusual for records show that the Torbay area was often a target for hit-and-run raiders. The controversy was the bombing of a military hospital and whether or not the building was displaying a conspicuous red cross. Here evidence seems to prove that it was. Post-war analysis of records show that Torquay was a favourite target for Luftwaffe pilots of the 10 Staffel of JG2 who lived in style at the Chateau de Louvigny and flew from their base at Carpiquet on the outskirts of Caen. From there it was a mere 170 miles across the Channel to Torbay, little more than 1/2 hour flying time.

It is known that in the summer of 1942 they were re-equipped with the FW 190 (shown above) a ground attack version of the FW190 similar to that used in the raid on the Palace Hotel. The bomb rack beneath the fuselage held a 500kg bomb.

It is to the hotel's great credit that they maintain a record of those historic days in a fine leather volume which includes photographs of patients and staff, the devastation, press cuttings and testimonials from former aircrew.

The raid of October 25th 1942 put the **Palace** out of commission for the rest of the war. It re-opened in March 1948 and many improvements have been made since those austere days. Today's visitors to this once again prestigious hotel would see little evidence of its dramatic past but for many aged and former wounded RAF aircrew it will always be the 'hospital' which to them was always a 'hotel'.

It was an ever aging band of veteran aircrew which, with the assistance of the East Devon Aircrew Association, in October 2007 saw the hotel arrange a 65th commemoration of the bombing   Over sixty members of the Association and their wives attended a commemorative service conducted at the hotel by the local vicar and this was followed by an excellent buffet provided by the management. Amongst those attending was the then President of the Aircrew Association, Air Marshal Sir Christopher Coville. Former patients making a return visit to the hotel included the previously mentioned Norman Conquer and Keith Lawrence with his wife, Kay.

However, that is not quite the end of the story for although the hotel had its excellent record book there was nothing to indicate to visitors its illustrious past.   This was rectified shortly after the 65th commemoration when, on behalf of the Aircrew Association, Paul Uphill, Managing Director of the Palace Hotel, (above left) was presented with a plaque by Grahame Holloway which depicted the RAF crest with the inscription 'RAF Hospital, Torquay. 1939-1942'.   It now hangs proudly in the hotel's entrance foyer.

The FIRST & LAST
The Royal Air Force in Devon & West Somerset

The Supermarine Southampton saw RAF service between 1925 - 1937 and flew from RAF Mountbatten, the service's first station in Devon.

The Westland Sea King, the only RAF aircraft still based in Devon, is flown by 'A' Flight, No.22 Squadron on Search and Rescue operations from former RAF Chivenor, which is now a Royal Marine Barracks.

The following pages will explore the presence of the RAF in Devon and West Somerset with short histories of operations from some sixteen stations listed in alphabetical order.

RAF BOLT HEAD

RAF Bolt Head was a small rudimentary airfield situated on a cliff-top site close to the small resort of Salcombe in the South Hams of Devon. It was one of a number of airfields constructed along the coast during WWII with the primary aim of giving aircraft operating away from their main bases a shorter distance to target areas in occupied Europe, thus giving a longer time to attack the enemy. Known as a Forward Operating Base (FOB), Bolt Head opened in 1941 for fighter squadrons from Nos.10 and 11 Groups. Their primary role was the escort of bombers attacking strategic targets in western France and, although never a major airfield; records show that during its four years of wartime operations no fewer that fourteen squadrons deployed aircraft from here, albeit not at the same time. Interestingly, the first aircraft to be permanently based there were two Lysanders detached from No. 276 Squadron.

The following year, 1942, as operational deployments increased, extra facilities were provided. These included blister hangars, two 'Sommerfield' track runways and bulk fuel storage together with barracks, flight and office accommodation. Unfortunately this work was spotted by the Luftwaffe who attacked with two Messerschmitt Bf109s on March 7th and hit a No.317 Squadron Spitfire as it was taking off. Luckily the pilot managed to land unhurt. It was given satellite status in the April of that year although it continued to be used as a FOB by Exeter based squadrons when engaged in escort or fighter sweep (Rhubarb) roles.

The main aircraft operating strikes from here were the Typhoon, Spitfire and, occasionally, the Mosquito. The station's closeness to the sea also gave rise to another role, that of Air Sea Rescue. Whilst ASR Spitfires would make sweeps to locate ditched aircrew the aircraft itself had no means of affecting a rescue. That task would fall to either high speed launches of amphibious aircraft such as the Supermarine Walrus operated by No.276 Squadron from Bolt Head during 1944.

The Hawker Typhoon.   The Supermarine Walrus.

After a rather inauspicious start, the Typhoon proved to be an excellent aircraft for high speed low level operations for which it was impressively armed with 20mm cannon and could carry up to eight 60lb rockets plus the ability to deliver two 1000lb bombs. It was at its peak during the D-day invasion when it delivered considerable damage to the German defence. Performance figures gave the Typhoon a top speed of 374 mph at 5,500 feet and in excess of 400 mph at 18,000 feet.

By contrast the Walrus cruised at a lowly 95 mph with a top speed of 135 mph. Interestingly, the prototype was designed by RJ Mitchell who is better known as the designer of the Spitfire. Fitted with a Bristol Pegasus engine mounted as a rearwards facing 'pusher' between the bi-plane's wings, its great advantage was the ability to land on water and vital in its Air Sea Rescue role which undoubtedly saved many aircrew from a watery grave. As war ended, Bolt Head was reduced to Care & Maintenance status at the end of April 1945 and finally closed two years later.

Today the airfield has reverted back to farmland. The remains of a few buildings may be seen together with a small strip of the former access track.

RAF CHIVENOR

Strategically situated in North Devon where the River Taw enters the Atlantic Ocean, RAF Chivenor started life in May 1940 when contractors moved onto level fields close to a pre-war grass airstrip. Three 3000 feet runways were quickly laid, a number of hangars and accommodation huts erected and the site officially became RAF Chivenor five months later on 1st October 1940.

Initially it became an Operational Conversion Unit (OCU) for Coastal Command aircrew when No.3 OCU arrived with their Blenheims, Ansons and Beauforts. It was also used during the following year by Nos. 252 and 272 Squadrons when they converted onto Beaufighters.

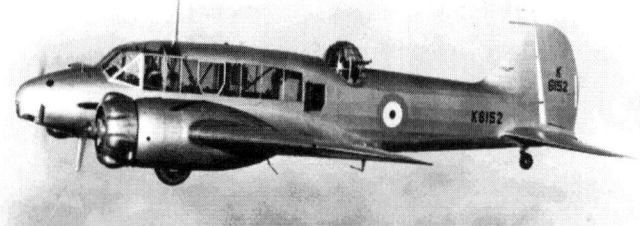

Above: An Avro Anson - an early arrival at Chivenor with No.3 OCU

In July 1941 No.3 OCU departed and No.5 OCU arrived with Wellingtons. However it was not until 1942 that squadrons arrived at Chivenor on a permanent basis, the first being No.172 with Wellingtons fitted with Leigh Lights. This highly powerful illumination system allowed searching aircraft to locate enemy U-boats during the hours of darkness when they surfaced to recharge batteries. The accolade for the first victory using this system fell to a Chivenor based Wellington on the 4th June 1942 when it surprised an Italian submarine which had surfaced in the Bay of Biscay.

Increased enemy U-boat activity necessitated a build-up of resources at Chivenor and initially these came in the form of the obsolete Whitleys of Nos.51 and 77 Squadrons.

Above: The Armstrong Whitworth Whitley

In May 1942, when the OCU left the station, Chivenor officially became part of No.19 Group Coastal Command, a status it retained until the end of hostilities. During the next three years various squadrons came and went and the types of aircraft seen in North Devon skies also changed. Perhaps the most significant came in February 1943 when No.59 Squadron arrived with their Fortress IIs, the first 4-engine bomber to use the airfield.

Unfortunately, the runways proved inadequate so their stay was a short one, their departure heralding the arrival of two more Wellington squadrons, one being No.407 (RCAF). However, later in the year there was a lull when activities temporarily moved to RAF St. Eval to enable repairs to Chivenor's runways to be carried out. These had taken heavy pounding through the incessant operations flown in the relentless war against the U-boat. Not only were enemy vessels destroyed at sea but so, too, were their main bases along the Atlantic coast of France. By the latter stages of the war operations from Chivenor were no longer required and its long period as a part of Coastal Command finally came to an end in October 1946 when it was transferred to Fighter Command.

This change of Command heralded a new beginning for Chivenor although this was not immediately recognised. The first aircraft to arrive, Mk.XVI Spitfires, Oxfords and Martinets, were not 'operational' but rather to be used for anti-aircraft co-operation duties. However, a number of subsequent changes occurred beginning with a training role when, in September 1947, it saw the arrival of No.208 Advanced Flying School (AFS). They stayed until early 1950 but then relocated to RAF Merryfield when the station was taken over by Transport Command. They had earmarked it for No.1 Overseas Ferry Unit but soon found the geographic location so far west did not suit their purpose so, once again, it reverted back to Fighter Command.

This was to be the last major change at Chivenor and began with the arrival of No.229 Operational Training Unit which provided the last stage of training for fast jet pilots before they joined front-line squadrons. For the next quarter of a century the sound of jet engines reverberated over the skies of North Devon heralding the dawn of the new jet age. As technology advanced so did Chivenor's aircraft and the local facilities to accommodate them. The earliest aircraft to arrive were Meteor 7s and Vampire FB5s. Before the training version of the Vampire, the T11, entered service in 1953, pilots would be introduced to jet flying with approximately three to four hours in the Meteor before their first flight in the single-seat Vampires.

Later these were phased out with the arrival of the Hawker Hunter, an aircraft designed as a replacement for the Meteor, the first one's being delivered to the RAF in 1954. Powered by a Rolls Royce Avon engine it had a top speed of 715 mph at sea level. By 1958 all RAF operational squadrons in Europe were equipped with the aircraft, the majority being the F6 version. The two seat training version, the T7, was issued to OCUs from August 1958.

A formation of Vampire T11's
WZ456, pictured nearest camera, has been flown by author.

The Hawker Hunter.

It is of interest to record that a number of Hunters are still flying, many having been restored by a Hunter Preservation Group at Exeter Airport. A tremendous roar accompanies their take-offs!

Activities from Chivenor further increased in June 1957 when a detachment of Sycamore helicopters arrived from No. 275 Squadron to undertake air-sea rescue duties. However, given the large area of the Bristol Channel they were expected to cover, their operational limitations restricted their effectiveness. As a result they were eventually replaced by the superior Whirlwind Mk.4 helicopter with the arrival of No.22 Squadron. In fact forty years later No.22 Squadron is still at Chivenor.

However, nothing is ever certain with the RAF and life at Chivenor was no exception. In September 1974 the OCU closed and the Hunters left. The RAF still retained control of the airfield with the helicopters of No.22 Squadron relocating to a new site at the edge of the airfield. They also re-equipped with a later version of the Whirlwind, the HAR 10 and, later still, the Wessex Mk.2. Providing air experience to ATC cadets also featured with the opening of No.624 Gliding School.

1975 saw a period of great uncertainty for Chivenor and, with only gliders and helicopters occupying a small part of the station, the Ministry of Defence permitted the use of the airfield by civil aircraft. Many plans were made for its future but all seemed to come to nothing. Perhaps this was just as well as in 1979 the RAF found that it needed additional facilities for Tactical Weapons training so a completely new re-building programme was undertaken and in August 1980 the first Hawks arrived with No.2 Tactical Weapons Unit. In addition to being used as an excellent training aircraft for the RAF the Hawk could also just as easily operate in a tactical role. Its great versatility made it a great favourite with air forces around the world and as a result it enjoyed a very strong export market. Domestically, the Hawk was to become the longest serving aircraft at Chivenor, remaining there until the RAF finally relinquished the station in October 1995.

Changing economic times and defence reviews has seen many cuts made in the resources of the RAF over the past twenty years and with this shrinkage the demand for pilots has grown ever less. With the decision to close Chivenor came the redeployment of the Hawks to RAF Valley on the Isle of Anglesey where a similar unit existed.

The Hawker Siddeley Hawk - the longest serving aircraft at RAF Chivenor

Today 'A' Flight of No.22 Squadron is still based in a corner of the former RAF Station which still hums with activity having a new role as a Royal Marine Barracks. No longer RAF Chivenor it is now RMB Chivenor!

The Westland Sea King, illustrated on page 28, is still operated by No.22 Squadron from Chivenor. Each year it saves countless lives after being called to emergencies involving visitors to the coasts of Devon and Cornwall and indeed further out to sea when fishing vessels, or larger ships, run into trouble through injured crew or more serious situations like shifting cargoes and sinking.

Despite the sterling service provided by the helicopters of 'A' Flight, No.22 Squadron, its future still remains in doubt with often muted plans to 'civilianise' the service. If that happens, the RAF will have left Chivenor for good.

RAF CULMHEAD

Originally known as RAF Church Stanton, RAF Culmhead made up the trio of RAF stations to be built in the Blackdown Hills which straddle the borders of Devon and Somerset. One of the earliest wartime stations, it was originally planned as an emergency landing ground but by the time it became operational in 1941 it had all the attributes of a fighter station with the standard triangular pattern runways. In fact this was borne out with the arrival of its first aircraft, two Polish fighter squadrons.

Part of No.2 Polish Fighter Wing, these were No.316 (Warsaw) Squadron and No.302 (Pozan) Squadron, both equipped with Hurricanes. However, No.302's stay was a very short one, only about a month, when they were replaced by No.306 (Torun) Squadron which brought Spitfires to the base. Their principal role was to provide defensive cover for Exeter and Bristol. However, when the Luftwaffe was quiet they would also provide aerial cover for convoys in home waters or escort our bombers making forays over the Brest Peninsula. It was a period when the station became known as 'The Polish Station'. The Poles left in June 1942 only to be replaced by another of our East European Allies, the Czechs. Their first Squadron, No.313 was soon joined by No.312 to form a Fighter Wing flying Spitfires. Their role at Church Stanton was similar to that undertaken by their predecessors and they remained at the station for around twelve months when the RAF arrived.

On the 22nd December 1943 RAF Church Stanton was renamed RAF Culmhead after one of Devon's longest rivers which rises nearby. The reason for the name change is said to have been to help the Americans who had recently moved into nearby RAF Dunkeswell and were getting confused by the number of other RAF stations with the word 'Church' in their name !

The next few months were a hive of activity at Culmhead with various Squadrons coming and going. These included Nos.131 and 165 which operated the Spitfire Mk.9 and in April 1944 the Royal Navy arrived with their No.610 Squadron as part of the Royal Navy's No.24 Fighter Wing. These were quickly bolstered by Nos.126, 131 and 616 Squadrons, the reasons for their appearance becoming evident two months later - on D-day, 6th June 1944.

This was a period when Culmhead pilots saw maximum action with numerous reconnaissance missions over Normandy prior to the invasion, followed by intensive action on D-day itself with strafing enemy aircraft, transport and troops. Within a week of the landings, the air and ground crews of Culmhead were on the move again, this time to hastily improvised landing strips in the newly liberated parts of France. One of the East Devon Aircrew Association's members, the late Roy Hook, who was one of the Spitfire pilots making the move, summed it up when he once said. *"We virtually lived out of suitcases, and in a period of sixteen months I was to fly from fifteen different airfields, many little more than grass strips."* One of the effects of constantly moving was that often personal records could not keep up with them. In Roy's case it was found that by November 1944 he had already flown in excess of one and half tours on operations without a break.

The switch of operations to mainland Europe ironically brought RAF Culmhead its greatest claim to fame. A month after D-day, in July 1944, the station became home for the RAF's first jet Squadron, No. 616 with the Gloster Meteor, the Allies first operational jet fighter. Culmhead was chosen for its isolated position in the Blackdown Hills, away from prying eyes. Here a greater degree of secrecy was possible in which to train aircrew on this new and revolutionary aircraft. Initially, only two aircraft arrived and the pilot of one of these was the late Clive Gosling, again a former member of the East Devon Aircrew Association. Clive was to become a highly experienced jet pilot and later chosen to fly a German Me.262, a twin engine jet fighter, which had fallen into Allied hands.

However, with initial pilots trained, the role of RAF Culmhead declined as the new jet squadrons departed to join the 2nd Tactical Air Force and operate from bases in Belgium, Holland and, later, Lubeck in Germany. As Clive once remarked:

"Life was tough. Not much water, you cleaned your teeth, washed and then shaved. If you did it in the wrong order you were in trouble. I flew a Meteor Mk.I back to the UK once to swap it for an improved Mk.3 which meant a stop in Brussels where I had my first bath for weeks. I drew a finger across my kneecap and it left a white line!"

Back at RAF Culmhead without operational aircraft the atmosphere had changed. A number of non-operational units moved in for short stays and were involved in such activities as target towing. No.10 Group Fighter Command was now keen to relinquish control and in December 1944 transferred its control to No.23 Group and it became a satellite airfield. For a short time gliding was carried on but by early 1945 this, too, had ceased and the station was put under 'care and maintenance', officially being transferred to Maintenance Command in August 1945. It closed a year later.

However, the site is not without activity and high radio masts and a sign 'Composite Signals Organisation' give an indication of current use but visitors are not welcome.

RAF DUNKESWELL

Dunkeswell had a very inauspicious start as a RAF Station due to the many construction problems encountered by George Wimpy, the main contractor, and its largely Irish workforce. Its opening as a RAF Station was delayed until 1942 when, initially, it was allocated to No.10 Group Fighter Command although because of the ongoing problems no squadron aircraft arrived.

By now, however, the war was entering another critical phase and the defence of the Atlantic Convoys bringing vital supplies to Britain was a high priority. Building delays were still continuing at Dunkeswell but, with rapidly shifting operational requirements, the RAF switched its role from an intended fighter station to the more urgent needs of No.19 Group Coastal Command. Three maritime squadrons were allocated to the station but the construction delays meant that, despite the high priority for increased Atlantic surveillance, hardly any flights took place during 1942.

Fortunately a dramatic change occurred the following year when, in July 1943, the Americans arrived. With a continuing build-up of their forces in Britain, and the need for permanent bases, RAF Dunkeswell was handed over to the US Navy to become the home of their No.7 Air Wing. Not only was it their only land base in Britain but the continuing build-up of resources was to also make it their largest in Europe.

Interestingly, despite being a US Naval Air Base, the first aircraft to arrive were Liberators from No.479 Anti-Submarine Group of the US Army Air Corps which until then had been operating from RAF St. Eval in Cornwall. However it was not long before these early models were replaced by the distinctive blue/grey PB4Y-1, the US Navy's specialised ant-submarine version.

Above: A Dunkeswell based PB4Y-1 Liberator

Also joining the Liberators at Dunkeswell was the Consolidated Catalina, shown below. An aircraft more frequently used over the oceans of the Southern Hemisphere, these were used both by the RAF and USN for long range surveillance and air-sea rescue operations.

Dunkeswell also became the base for a Royal Navy flight of six Spitfires but, although operating under Royal Navy markings, they were in fact flown by US Navy pilots. Adding to the variety of aircraft using the base were B-17 Flying Fortresses of the USAAF who used it on an occasional basis.

As soon as the war in Europe ended the US forces wasted no time in departing from Dunkeswell, leaving by the end of July 1945. At the time it was reported there were seventy Liberators to be repatriated. Thirty-six left for the US but the remaining thirty-four were regarded as surplus to US requirements and were offered to the British Government for the bargain price of $500 each. However, with so many surplus aircraft, the Government made a counter offer of $50 per aircraft. It was an offer the US thought so derisory that they scrapped them!

With the departure of the Americans, on the 6th August 1945 it reverted to RAF command and transferred to No.46 Group Transport Command. It then became home to No.3 Overseas Aircraft Preparation Unit and No.16 Ferry Unit. Their role was to prepare and ferry various aircraft surplus to our requirements to the Middle East or foreign air forces. This was fulfilled by March 1946 when the airfield was downgraded to 'Care & Maintenance' and the RAF finally left in February 1949.

Today flying still takes place at Dunkeswell which operates as a civil airfield with a local flying club and is also a popular base for parachute enthusiasts. A reminder of its former days as a formidable US Navy base remains in the form of a propeller shaped memorial, whilst in an adjacent industrial park will be found a 'Memorial Museum' which houses many artefacts from those days. Dunkeswell still remains a place of pilgrimage for the now aging US veterans who were once stationed there and a 'Book of Remembrance' will be found in the US corner of the nearby parish church. In it is the name of Lt. Joseph Kennedy, the brother of JFK the former American President. He arrived at Dunkeswell in 1943 and later volunteered for a top secret but dangerous mission code named 'Project Anvil'. Flying from Dunkeswell to a base in Norfolk, he and his co-pilot took off in a new Liberator laden with 20,000lbs of H.E. bound for an enemy V-1 site. Sadly the aircraft blew up shortly after crossing the English coast and both men were killed.

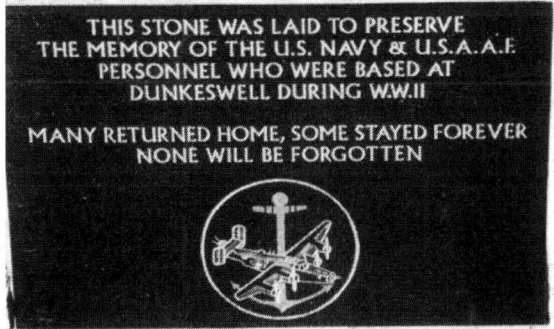

Above: The Dunkeswell Memorial and its inscription.

In recent years the South West Airfields Heritage Trust has arranged the occasional Air Day at Dunkeswell when some of the airfield's historic aircraft have made a return.

The USAAF B-17 Flying Fortress, featured above, made its appearance in June 1993. Also making appearances have been a Catalina and a B-24 Liberator with the nick-name 'Diamond Lil '.

RAF EXETER

Exeter had one great advantage when war was declared in September 1939 in that it was already an established airport, albeit with long grass runways. It was an asset quickly realised by the Air Ministry who immediately requisitioned it for the Royal Air Force and a research team moved in from Farnborough to undertake trials on how to disable barrage balloons. Civil flying still continued, with Jersey Airlines providing an important link to the Channel Islands until they became occupied by the Germans in June 1940. The same month the RAF's first operational aircraft arrived.

These were the Hurricanes of No.213 Squadron, followed a couple of weeks later, on the 5th July 1940, by the arrival of further Hurricanes with No.87 Squadron. The pilots of both squadrons were no strangers to conflict; all being battle-hardened veterans who had provided aerial cover during the withdrawal of our troops from Dunkirk. The day following, the 6th July 1940, saw the arrival of No.87 Squadron and, with all civil operations having ceased, the airfield officially became RAF Exeter and construction work for additional buildings started.

Soon Exeter's aircraft were to be engaged in what we now know as the 'Battle of Britain'. Their role was to protect the region, and particularly the naval bases at Devonport and Portland, from enemy attack. This brought them into considerable contact with the enemy as the naval bases were prime targets. No.87 Squadron's first 'kill' has been recorded as being on the 11th July 1940, shortly after their arrival at Exeter, although other details of this encounter are sketchy. Two weeks later a Heinkel 111 bomber became prey to Exeter's Hurricanes when it was shot down near Smeatharpe.

August 1940 was, in many respects, to be Exeter's busiest month of war and one when the 'Battle of Britain' was at its height. On the 11th fourteen Hurricanes from Nos.87 and 213 Squadrons were scrambled to defend Portland naval base against an enemy force estimated to be 165 strong and comprising Ju88's and He111's with an escort of Bf109E's and Bf110's.

The Exeter pilots claimed shooting down two of the enemy's bomber force before becoming embroiled with their fighter escort. Here they claimed damaging five but not without loss. Both Nos.87 and 213 Squadrons lost two Hurricanes each with the death of three of their pilots. The following day Hurricanes of No.213 Squadron were sent to intercept a raid on Portsmouth Dockyard but, although claiming shooting down two Ju88's, they lost another two of their aircraft and pilots. Seemingly there was no respite for, the third day running, they were sent eastwards once again to protect Portsmouth and Southampton. Although again making claims, now of three 'kills', both squadrons were to lose another pilot. A day of inactivity followed but on the 15th both squadrons were again scrambled and again lost another three pilots, one from No.213 squadron and two from No.87. Further losses came on the 25th when in the defence of Portland No.87 Squadron lost another three aircraft and their pilots although they claimed four more enemy aircraft had been destroyed.

Later that year, in November, No.87 Squadron departed with its Hurricanes and No.263 Squadron arrived with a new aircraft for the Devonshire skies, the Whirlwind. This was a highly manoeuvrable aircraft and the first single-seat, twin-engine, fighter to be flown by the RAF and Exeter being the first station to see its deployment. It also had a slight speed advantage over the Hurricanes it replaced.

Above: The Westland Whirlwind, an aircraft which was operated by No.263 Squadron from Exeter between November 1940 and April 1941

With the departure of the Whirlwinds, No.66 Squadron arrived with Exeter's first Spitfires. However 1941 was also the year when Exeter saw the beginning of many further squadron changes. Many operated either Hurricanes or Spitfires but often they stayed only for a short time, usually just long enough to complete a particular task such as convoy protection patrols. 1941 also saw a number of Luftwaffe raids on airfield with five during the early months of the year. The worst of these was on April 5th when it was attacked by three enemy bombers which came in low over the coast, their bombs demolishing a hangar, damaging sixteen unspecified aircraft and completely wrecking a Wellington. Later that month, on the 26th, No.307 Squadron arrived.

This squadron was fundamentally different from all which had previously served at Exeter. It was Polish and with No.317 Squadron, which arrived in the July, was to form part of No.2 Polish Fighter Wing. They were equipped with the Boulton Paul Defiant which was used in a night fighter role. In fact No.307 Squadron was to remain at Exeter until April 1943, the longest period that any operational Squadron served there during the war. Despite particularly bad weather they played an important part in defending Exeter during the 1942 *Baedecker* raids.

May of that year also saw the arrival of another specialist night fighter squadron, No.247, which was equipped with Typhoons.

The Boulton Paul Defiant

By now changes at Exeter were so rapid it was difficult to keep count of the various squadrons and aircraft which included the Beaufighter and Mosquito. Although basically a fighter station in the latter part of 1942, and continuing through 1943, Exeter was also occasionally used as a forward base for No.2 Bomber Group operations. When the Americans joined forces it was not unusual to see such aircraft as the A-20 Havoc, P-38 Lightning and the P-47 Thunderbolt in local skies. Occasionally, too, the Royal Navy was in evidence when Swordfish of No. 834 Squadron flew night operations in search of enemy E-boats in the Channel. They recorded some success in the June when they attacked a group of E-boats off the Channel Islands.

However, April 1944 saw one of the biggest changes at Exeter during the war when the RAF suddenly moved out, the Americans moved in, and Exeter became Station 463 of the USAAF. Of course what was not known by the general population at the time were the Allied plans for the liberation of occupied Europe. On the 18th April 1944 four squadrons of the 440th Transport Carrier Group, 50th Troop Carrier Wing, arrived with their complement of forty five C-47 aircraft together with a number of Hadrian

Gliders. Immediately intensive exercises commenced which, as we now know, culminated with airborne troops participating in the Normandy landings on D-day, the 6th June 1944. It was an operation in which, as we shall see later, other local airfields participated.

During these run-up operations the Exeter Canal and the River Exe played an important role as a mirror image of the Caen Canal and the River Orne in Normandy. A memorial plaque situated on the banks of the canal on the Exeter side of the Countess Wear cantilever bridge records the events.

The memorial plaque at the Countess Wear canal bridge.

Post D-day, activities at Exeter greatly decreased. The airfield still remained under USAAF control until the 20th November 1944, used mainly as a base for an airborne ambulance service repatriating wounded US troops back to the UK. In the latter weeks of 1944, after Exeter had returned to RAF control, 'A' Flight of No.275 Squadron moved in with their Walrus amphibians although on their departure in early 1945 the station was transferred to No.23 (Training) Group for use as a glider training school. They were equipped with Master II tugs and Hotspur gliders. However in July 1945, after the war in Europe had ended, RAF Exeter once again reverted back to Fighter Command. Later No.601 Squadron arrived with

Oxfords, Hurricanes and Vengeances, followed by the Spitfires of No.329 (French) Squadron. This unit was disbanded in November 1945 and on the 1st January 1947 the airfield was returned to the Ministry of Civil Aviation. However, this did not end a RAF presence for the RAFVR No.10 Reserve Flying School opened there in May 1949, remaining until June 1954 when it was closed due to armed forces cut-backs. During its five years of operation its reserve pilots initially flew Tiger Moths and Ansons, both later replaced by Chipmunks. The author was one of the pilots attached to No.10 RFS which also at that time would occasionally provide flights for ATC cadets.

With a much longer post-war stay at Exeter was No. 3 Civilian Anti-Aircraft Co-operation Unit (CAACU) which was formed at the airfield in March 1951. It was an interesting unit in so much that all the pilots were reservists, the aircraft were all RAF but types which had basically reached the end of squadron service and they were maintained by civilians. Their role was to provide sorties for trainee Fighter Controllers and calibration and target towing for the Army and Royal Navy, basically tasks which the RAF no longer wished to undertake. CAACU remained at Exeter for just over twenty years, finally being disbanded at the end of 1971. It was a period which saw a wide variety of aircraft at Exeter, ranging from Spitfires and Beaufighters in the very early days, to Oxfords, Mosquitoes and Balliols before entering the jet age with Vampires, Meteors and, finally, Hunters.

A Balliol flown by CAACU at Exeter in 1957

With the disbandment of CAACU only one minor RAF presence remained, namely No.4 Air Experience Flight. Filling the gap left by the closure of No.10 RFS in 1954, it opened in 1958 to provide air experience flights for ATC Cadets. Operating Chipmunks, the unit survived until the mid -1990's.

Today Exeter's airport is thriving with 'International' added to its name. It is popular with many airlines which operate holiday charter flights throughout the year. However, by far the airport's greatest user is FlyBe, Europe's largest regional airline, and one whose pedigree dates back to pre-war Jersey Airlines followed by 'Jersey European Airways' and 'British European'. Although its aircraft are based throughout the UK its headquarters are at Exeter and include a large aero-engineering complex.

However, the airport's significant wartime heritage has not been forgotten and, at the time of writing, plans are in hand to commemorate this with a life size statue of a Hurricane pilot, gazing skywards for returning comrades. A mould has already been prepared for its ultimate casting in bronze. It is also understood that the base will contain details of all the squadrons which served there during WWII. Donations towards its cost have come from many sources, not least from the Polish Air Force Association in recognition of the role their airmen played during the airfield's wartime days.

RNAS HALDON - HMS HERON II

Situated on the top of the Haldon Hills this is one of Devon's oldest airfields. Records show that in 1928 an Avro 594 Avian was purchased by William Parkhouse, the then airfield owner, and at that time it was used for events such as 'Flying Circuses' or 'Air Pageants'. A period as a commercial airfield followed from the spring of 1933 when a small airline, known as GWR Air Services, started a twice-weekly service between Plymouth's Roborough airfield and Cardiff, with an interim stop at Haldon. They had one aircraft, a Westland Wessex, which was chartered from Imperial Airways. The following year Provincial Airways included a Haldon stop on their route from Croydon to Plymouth via Southampton. Their aircraft was the De Havilland Dragon, a forerunner of the Rapide. In January 1937 the Straight Corporation took control of the airfield.

It has been included in the book as pre-war the RAF had occasionally used the site whilst undertaking aircraft trials and two aircraft recorded as having made a visit were the Fairey IIIF, a general purpose 2-seat bi-plane which entered RAF service in 1927, and the Vickers Virginia which entered the RAF in 1925 as a heavy night bomber. This was probably the largest aircraft to land at the airfield. After the outbreak of war Haldon was first requisitioned by the Air Ministry and occasionally used by aircraft from RAF Boscombe Down whilst carrying out exercises in Lyme Bay. However with little real use for it, the Air Ministry transferred it to the Admiralty and on the 18th August 1941 it became a satellite of HMS Heron, Yeovilton, and named in naval fashion as HMS Heron II.

Most of the activity at Haldon comprised target-towing aircraft from Nos.761 and 794 Squadrons and operational requirements proved minimal. There was also an environmental problem as its high coastal location often resulted in cancelled operations due to either high winds or coastal fog. As a result the base was reduced to Care and Maintenance status in May 1943.

One member of the East Devon Aircrew Association who can recollect its early use by the Royal Navy is former naval pilot Dick Allen of Exton. At the end of December 1942 he was posted to No.762 Fighter Training Squadron based at RNAS, Yeovilton, and arrived at Haldon to serve a short detachment whilst undertaking gunnery training off Teignmouth. The squadron operated Fairey Fulmar and Miles Martinet aircraft. Now a nonagenarian, when asked if he could recall his experiences at Haldon he replied:

"The facilities were extremely limited with nothing more than a few huts. Fortunately, as aircrew, we were looked after quite well and were billeted in a large hotel at the end of Teignmouth Sea Front from where we were taken to the airfield by bus each morning. As for incidents there were none really because our flying was basically a continuation of weapons training.

However we did have one notable event although not involving any of our aircraft. An American Air Force P-38 Lightning had struck the sea whilst low flying off the French coast and had lost a propeller. For some reason the pilot decided to land at Haldon on his one good engine and, to be honest, it was travelling at some speed and with the being airfield so small we did not think the pilot would make it. However, we had not reckoned on the aircraft's tricycle undercarriage which was fairly new to us. As soon as he touched down the pilot slammed on the brakes and, to our amazement, the aircraft came to a rapid halt. Other than that my short stay at the airfield was relatively excitement free."

The Fulmar, which entered squadron service in June 1940, was the first 8-gun fighter to be operated by the Royal Navy, its armament giving it the same fire-power as the Spitfire and Hurricane. Although powered by a Rolls Royce Merlin VIII engine, its larger size and two-man crew meant its top speed was only 256 mph. It was also no match in other respects.

The Fairey Fulmar which flew from Haldon in 1942

Post war the site returned to private ownership and by the late 1960's part was once again being used by golfers, the rest reverting to scrub. Today, other than the remains of the former club house located amid the scrub near Little Haldon Cross, you would be hard pushed to find any tangible evidence of its early flying history. However, this is not to say it has been forgotten for a simple plaque set in a granite block records those early days and will be found close to the car park on the East side of the main road.

RAF HARROWBEER

Returning to West Devon we now visit the site of former RAF Harrowbeer which is situated close to the village of Yelverton on Dartmoor's western fringe. The station first opened in August 1941 and those accessing the site via the road behind the 'Leg 'O Mutton' inn will find the granite memorial stone illustrated below.

The inscription reads:
"RAF Harrowbeer. Operational 1941 - 1949.

From this station flew pilots of many Commonwealth and Allied countries, including Britain, Canada, Czechoslovakia, France, Poland, Southern Rhodesia and the USA, with the support of the ground crews and airfield defence units. This stone is in memory of all those who served here and especially those who gave their lives. Many local residents helped build and maintain this airfield. Unveiled by the first Station Commander, Group Captain the Hon E.F. Ward on the 15th August 1981, the fortieth anniversary of the opening of this station."

On opening it was initially designated as a fighter station under the control of No.10 Group Fighter Command and a satellite of RAF Exeter. During the war no fewer than seventeen different squadrons operated from the airfield, including two from the Fleet Air Arm. It was also a temporary home to pilots of many nations as the memorial plaque indicates. One of the first squadrons to arrive was the RAF's No.130 Squadron which operated the Spitfire Mk V with a primary role of escorting our bombers on raids across the Channel and also providing air cover for our own shipping. However their stay was short, only lasting during October and November. Following their departure two further Spitfire squadrons arrived, namely No.302 (Polish) Squadron and No.312 (Czech) Squadron. Another stalwart of the Battle of Britain, the Hurricane, also briefly operated from here during 1942 when No.175 Squadron was based here for a short period. By late 1942, however, it was changing from a predominantly fighter base to that of a more versatile fighter-bomber role engaged on anti-shipping strikes.

The Hawker Hurricane (above) occasionally operated from RAF Harrobeer.

These missions can be illustrated by the work of No.193 Squadron which undertook a variety of roles with their Typhoons. These included the interception of Luftwaffe 'intruder' patrols as well as making their own 'rhubarb' sweeps on predominately rail and airfield targets in Northern France. In early 1943 their Typhoons were joined by Whirlwinds of No.263 Squadron which re-located from Exeter.

By now the Harrowbeer based squadrons had another vital role, namely attacking the newly constructed V-1 sites in Northern France. Here the Typhoons of No's.193 and 266 Squadrons were invaluable with their ability to conduct low level strikes against the well-hidden V-1 sites.

With its proximity to the sea, Harrowbeer also acquired another important task, that of Air Sea Rescue. Older model Spitfires, such as the Mk.III flown by No.276 Squadron between 1941-44, would make 'sweeps' across the Channel to locate 'downed' aircrew, an operation similar to that described earlier from RAF Bolt Head.

Following D-day, and with the Allied advance through France firmly established, the base was temporarily reduced to Care & Maintenance status although it still remained open for operational flying by Communications Flight aircraft. However in January 1945 it reopened for more extensive use by fighter squadron detachments, anti-aircraft co-operation units and, in late 1947, by No.19 Communications Flight which transferred from Roborough. One of the aircraft they flew was the Avro Anson. Mk XIX featured below.

It was much used by Communications Flights such as that of No.19 Flight during their stay at Harrowbeer between December 1947 and August 1948.

Eventually the RAF vacated the airfield in the summer of 1948 following which there was a heated debate as to its future use. Many saw the large concrete runways providing a sound base for a new airport for the City of Plymouth. The Ministry of Civil Aviation put forward proposals but these raised strong opposition from conservationists. Their argument was based on the fact the airfield had been constructed within the Dartmoor National Park and therefore should revert to its natural state as common land. In the end the conservationists won the day.

Today the former airfield is a popular leisure area comprising a mix of gorse and moorland pasture. However remnants of its historic role during WWII still remain and sections of runway are clearly visible together with the perimeter track along which many of the aircraft dispersal bays have been preserved and are frequently used as shelter by those enjoying a picnic.

Of buildings remaining, part of what was the control tower area is now occupied by the Knightstone Tea Rooms. Its proprietor, Michael Hayes, is a keen collector of aviation 'bits and pieces' and has a considerable collection in his private museum. Occasionally, too, he arranges living history events adjacent to the tea rooms whilst nearby one of the airfield's WWII air raid shelters has been renovated and will be opened to the public on special occasions.

RAF MERRYFIELD

Situated near the small Somerset village of Ilton, between Taunton and Ilminster, construction of former RAF Merryfield began in 1942 when it was originally known as RAF Isle Abbots. With a typical three runway configuration it was originally planned as a bomber station but, as completion neared, in April 1943 it was earmarked as a suitable base for future use by the USAAF. In September 1943 its name changed to Merryfield but it did not officially open until February 1944 when substantial numbers of the US forces started to arrive. By the April it was home to four squadrons of the USAAF 441st TCG, 50th TCW, IXth Troop Carrier Command with their C-47's and Hadrian gliders. Intensive training followed and by the end of May reports show that they were highly efficient at rapid hook-ups and deployment.

In keeping with other South West airfields, the location of Merryfield made it an ideal launch pad for D-day, 6th June 1944, when airborne forces led the way for the beachhead landings. Those from Merryfield had a leading role in delivering the 82nd and 101st US Airborne Divisions behind enemy lines, close to St. Mere Eglise on the Cherbourg Peninsula, to capture strategic road and rail bridges to facilitate later advances from the beaches. With the airborne assault now complete, another important role came to the station a month later, in July, when the 61st Field Hospital was established there. A large tented area with an ambulance park, it received battlefield casualties flown in by the US 813 Air Evacuation Transport Squadron. At the same time the airfield reverted back to RAF No.10 Group Fighter Command although the Americans remained until the November. However No.10 Group's tenure was short for at the end of the month it was transferred yet again, this time to 47 Group, Transport Command.

During the next twelve months there seemed to be much 'coming and going' at the station as it switched between a transport version of the Halifax bomber, Dakotas, Liberators and Stirlings. In the early stages much of this activity was centred on supplies to the Far East where operations still continued against the Japanese. One of the squadrons operating the Stirling was No.242 which, whilst at Merryfield, converted to the Avro York. East Devon Aircrew Association member Glyn Roberts was a navigator with the squadron at the time and his reminiscences appear later in the book.

However, by October 1946 there was no further any operational need for the station and therefore it was closed with its status reduced to that of a reserve airfield. It may have eventually been disposed of completely had it not been for the Korean War and the need for more training facilities. It was re-opened by Flying Training Command in November 1951 as No.208 AFS (Advanced Flying School). Here pilots had their first experience of flying jet aircraft in current operational squadron service.

Arriving at Merryfield in 1952 was Grahame Holloway, this book's author and one of the aircraft he flew from there was WR264, the Vampire FB9 shown above. He recalls that there were two training squadrons, one still equipped with a number of the early Mk. FI Vampires although most on the station were the then current FB5 and FB9 (Fighter Bomber) versions, the latter being a tropical version for service in the Middle and Far East. At the time of his arrival a pilot's first experience of jet flying came in the dual-control

59

Meteor Mk7 then, after 3 to 4 hours acclimatisation, it was solo in the single seat Vampire. However this changed in early 1953 with the arrival of a trainer version of the Vampire, the dual-control T11.

With the Korean War over, the need for training facilities diminished and in February 1955 these ceased at Merryfield although it became operationally active again within two months with its transfer to No.1 Group Bomber Command and the arrival of No.231 OCU with its photo-reconnaissance versions of the Canberra. They remained for over a year but the low standard of aids at the station led to their departure in November 1956.

Although now in a state of limbo as far as the RAF was concerned, aircraft movements continued at the station. As far back as 1949 the Westland Aircraft Co, Ltd. had been using the airfield for the testing of its military products, starting with the Westland Wyvern for the Royal Navy. They also air tested a number of aircraft repaired at Yeovil and these included Meteors and Sabres. Also in November 1956 the Royal Navy moved their Sea Venoms of No.788 Squadron from Yeovilton whilst reconstruction was being carried out. However, when they left in January 1958 Merryfield reverted to 'Care and Maintenance'.

Throughout the 1960's Merryfield grew into a state of decay, being occupied at times by 'travellers'. However respite came in the early 70's when, once again, the Royal Navy took an interest and, re-building part of the infrastructure, reopened it in May 1972 as HMS Heron, RNAS Merryfield, and a satellite for their main base at RNAS Yeovilton.

RAF MOUNT BATTEN

The first recorded military aerial activity in Devon appears be during the First World War when the Royal Navy saw its potential and added to its presence at Devonport by initially operating small airships from a site where the River Plym enters the Sound. This was known as RNAS Cattedown. However, on the 1st October 1929 the Royal Navy transferred the facilities to the Royal Air Force when it became known as RAF Mount Batten.

Plymouth has long been a site of strategic importance to the military, particularly the Royal Navy. Its excellent anchorage afforded by the safe haven of Plymouth Sound has witnessed many notable occasions through the centuries and most schoolboys will have heard the story of how Sir Francis Drake insisted on finishing his game of bowls on Plymouth Hoe before sailing out to defeat the giant Spanish Armada which greatly outnumbered his own fleet.

It also played an important role in the Civil War when it became a stronghold for Parliament. However when the monarchy was restored with the return of Charles II he left the city with a legacy reminding them never to turn against the Crown again. This was in the form of a giant citadel which not only looked out towards the sea but also the city. The aim was two-fold, the protection of the city against invaders from the sea but also cannons which could face the local population if they ever thought of rising against him. The citadel is still very much a military establishment today and occupied by the Army.

The arrival of the Royal Air Force in 1929 saw increasing use of seaplanes, initially Supermarine's Southampton and Scapa and, later, the Saunders-Roe London. The former, which first flew in 1925, arrived at RAF Mount

Batten shortly after it opened in 1929 when it was allocated to No.204 Squadron.

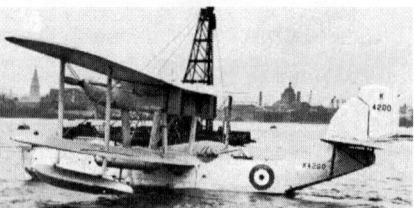

The Supermarine Southampton   The Supermarine Scapa

The Supermarine Southampton was designed for coastal reconnaissance. It was designed by R.J. Mitchell, who later designed the iconic Spitfire, and was powered by two 502 h.p. Napier Lion engines which gave it a cruising speed of 83 mph and a range of 930 miles. As well as with UK based squadrons, including No.204 at Mountbatten, it also saw service with RAF Squadrons in Iraq and Singapore. In 1936 the squadron was re-equipped with the newer Saunders-Roe London, the Southampton being finally retired from service in September 1937.

A great improvement on the Southampton was the Scapa which was also built by Supermarine. Of all-metal construction it entered service with the RAF in 1932 and was powered by two 525 hp Rolls Royce Kestrel engines which gave it a top speed of 141 mph at 3000 feet. Intended for general reconnaissance duties, the Scapa had a crew of five and its first deployment in the UK was with No.204 Squadron at RAF Mount Batten in August 1935. It was finally withdrawn from front-line squadrons in 1938 as the storm clouds over Europe were gathering.

Arriving at No. 204 Squadron a year after the Scapa, in October 1936, was the Sanders-Roe London. In fact the Mount Batten based squadron was the first to receive the aircraft and there was much publicity the following year when their aircraft undertook a flight to New South Wales, Australia, and back. For this journey the aircraft were fitted with long-range fuel tanks which more than doubled their normal range of 1100 miles to 2600. Powered by two Bristol Pegasus X radial engines of 1000 hp each, it had a cruising speed of just under 130 mph and a top speed of 155 mph. At the outbreak of WWII the RAF still had twenty-nine in operation with No.202 Squadron based in Gibraltar operating them until 1941.

The Saunders-Roe London

The outbreak of war in September 1939 saw rapid changes in the development of aircraft with only a few which had been developed pre-war actually serving with distinction. Immediately coming to mind is the Spitfire but equally outstanding in its own specialist role was the Short Sunderland which first entered RAF service in 1938.

It was an aircraft which was to see sterling service from RAF Mount Batten throughout the war. Re-equipping No.204 Squadron, it also served with other Plymouth squadrons of which, perhaps, the best remembered is No.10 Squadron of the Royal Australian Air Force. Part of RAF No.19 Group, Coastal Command, their aircraft flew no fewer than 3177 sorties over the hostile Atlantic and Bay of Biscay. However, their tally of seven U-boats confirmed sunk, plus many damaged, was not without loss. Nineteen of their aircraft were to be lost to the enemy and a further six in unfortunate accidents before the squadron returned home to Australia in October 1945.

The above photograph is one of the few which remain of a No.10 Squadron Sunderland moored at RAF Mount Batten.

Despite the losses incurred by No.10 Squadron, and others, the Sunderland was a heavily defended aircraft, so much so that it was nicknamed the 'Flying Porcupine' by the enemy. Its proven success for maritime operations resulted in a number of variants being built, the last being the Mk V which entered squadron service in February 1945. Powered by four 1200 hp Pratt and Whitney Wasp engines, the aircraft had a top speed of 213 mph at 5000 feet and had a normal crew complement of eleven. After the war the Sunderland also saw service during the Berlin Airlift, in Korea and against terrorists in Malaya before eventually being withdrawn in 1959. In fact the last flight of the RAF's last Sunderland was officially made from Singapore on the 20th May 1959 where it had been serving with No.205 Squadron.

Although the era of flying boats at Mount Batten came to a gradual end after the war it did not mean an end to RAF activities for it then operated as the RAF School of Combat Survival and Rescue, an essential part of aircrew training. It also continued as an important base for the RAF Marine Craft Unit which operated its high speed launches in a variety of roles. Whilst most of the activities of this special unit have centred on its hazardous missions of rescuing shot-down airmen from the sea during WWII, its origins are much older and can be traced back to 1918 when the RAF was first formed.

The Marine Branch saw many changes with the passage of time and the early pinnaces were replaced by sleeker, faster vessels as war progressed. These high speed rescue launches were strategically placed in harbours around the coast which locally included Exmouth and Plymouth.

HSL 193, (above), was initially one of the two launches based at Exmouth but was moved to RAF Mount Batten in 1944, shortly before D-day.

RTTL 2757 (above), also based at RAF Mount Batten, was one of the new post-war launches built by Vosper Ltd of Portsmouth to reflect the changing needs of the RAF.   Entering service in 1957, her two Rolls Royce Sea

65

Griffin engines gave her a speed of 39 knots (approx 45 mph). She had a crew of nine and as well as rescue work she was also used for target towing. She was based at Plymouth twice, the first for a short spell in 1965-66 and again from 1971-77.

However she has found a special niche in RAF history for on the 26th November 1977 she left Plymouth for a 23 hour voyage to the Royal Victoria Docks in London from where she was transported to the RAF Museum at Hendon as a permanent memorial to the work of the RAF Marine Craft Units.

However, arguably, RAF Mount Batten's most important peace-time role was that as the Maritime Headquarters and Air-Sea Rescue co-ordination Centre. Here rescue missions throughout most of the Western Hemisphere would be co-ordinated, many involving the long-range Nimrod surveillance aircraft then stationed at RAF St. Mawgan in Cornwall. Later cut-backs and economics led to the re-deployment of the Nimrods to Scotland and with their departure the co-ordination centre also moved northwards bringing the RAF's long association with Mount Batten to an end in 1992.

RAF OKEHAMPTON (Folly Gate).

The wild moors of Dartmoor have provided training grounds for the military since the mid-19th century so in some respects it was not surprising to find an airfield existed on level ground close to its northern fringe. It was situated just north of Okehampton adjoining the eastern side of the A386 main road at the village of Folly Gate.

Never an airfield of any great substance, it is known to have existed since 1928 when it was used annually, usually during the summer months, as an Army Co-operation base during artillery exercises on the high moor. Nos. 13 and 16 Squadrons were the main users and they operated the Bristol F2B and, later, the Hawker Audax. Their crews slept in tents on the airfield.

Left: The Hawker Audax, used during artillery exercises on Dartmoor

By the summer of 1939 these aircraft had been replaced by Lysanders but the field still lacked facilities of any kind and, even after the outbreak of war, no material change took place until August 1940. However, subsequent to the outbreak of hostilities its use was slowly expanded and there is a record that in August 1940 a reformed No.16 Squadron arrived with their Lysanders having received severe casualties whilst operating in France. On arrival they commenced dawn and dusk coastal patrols over an area covering the Bristol Channel from Barnstaple to Portishead and also, to the South, Lyme Bay. However, by late autumn the notoriously fickle Dartmoor weather was making itself felt and the unit redeployed to Harrowbeer.

Eventually, in May 1941, it became a satellite of Weston Zoyland, a Somerset airfield, but never a major airfield in its own right. From March 1942 it was used by No.73 Maintenance Unit for holding spares, although Army Co-operation detachments still occasionally visited with their Lysanders and Austers so, too, did the US Army with Piper Cubs. Some elderly locals maintain that the field was also used as an explosives store.

Never other than a grass field, today the land has been returned to private ownership and is currently used as pasture. It is left largely to one's imagination as to the field's facilities although locals graphically describe how Nissen huts once stood where the row of houses facing the main road now stand. However according to local information, there is one legacy remaining and that is the Folly Gate village hall, since enlarged and improved it was once the former NAAFI.

Above: Two of the aircraft operating at Folly Gate between 1939-1942. Left is a Lysander used for patrolling the Bristol Channel and Lyme Bay. Right, is an Army Air Corps Auster used for artillery spotting on Dartmoor.

RAF POLTIMORE

This former small, but extremely important, RAF Station lies only a couple of miles from Exeter airport on the eastern fringe of the city at Poltimore Park, the grounds of a former 17th century stately home. Opening in 1942, it was soon to play a pivotal role in the defence of the West Country as the Sector Operations Room for RAF No.10 Fighter Group. With the main operations room built underground, it was here that WAAF operators would receive reports from the area's radar stations, plus the Royal Observer Corps, and from their information plot the position of incoming raiders on large map tables. This information would then allow the Duty Controller to 'scramble' appropriate squadrons to intercept the intruders.

This old photograph shows plotters at Poltimore in 1942.

However Poltimore also controlled many operations which were more routine. These ranged from escorting convoys as they progressed through the Channel to providing fighter escorts for bombers carrying out raids on enemy naval facilities on the French Atlantic coast.

For most pilots missions comprised fighter sweeps across the Channel, finding targets of choice. These ranged from enemy shipping off the Normandy and Brittany coasts to destroying their transport links and military installations on the ground. Later, these sweeps, also known by the pilots as 'Rhubarbs' , increased in intensity as D-Day approached and, during the invasion itself, Poltimore was to play an increasingly important part in co-ordinating air strikes and cover for the landing forces.

Understandably as the Allies advanced across Europe the role of Poltimore diminished and, no longer required post-war, it closed in 1946.   But, surprisingly, it was soon to find another role.   The competition between the Western Allies and the Soviet Union for influence in post-war Europe grew ever more tense, escalating into what became known as the 'Cold War'. At times it seemed that war could erupt between the opposing sides, both of which had considerable military force at their disposal. For many years even nuclear war seemed likely and in the UK plans were rapidly drawn up to protect the civilian population should this occur.

It is at this point that a fundamental change in the role of the ROC began to take place.   During the war its small operational HQ had been in Exeter then, after hostilities ceased, it moved to share the facilities at the RAF radar station on the marshes at Exminster.   By now, however, the threat of a nuclear war which had brought about a radical re-think for the nation's defence also saw a dramatic revival in the role of the ROC. Gone were the old aircraft recognition training sessions and "spotting' duties. Out, too, went the surface built observation posts. The nuclear age had arrived and these old posts were superseded by small underground bunkers which could accommodate up to a dozen men whilst a number of major control centres were strategically placed around the country.

New equipment was provided which could monitor nuclear bomb bursts, ascertain their yield and, given the prevailing wind conditions, plot areas of radioactive fall-out. This information would then be passed through a warning system to ensure the civilian population took protective cover.

In the 1950's the site at Poltimore was expanded to become HQ of No.10 Group ROC which covered much of the West Country. Additions included a large bomb-proof operations centre which was built adjacent to the existing WWII huts. These remained in situ for use by ROC administration staff and access to the wartime underground operations centre was effectively sealed off and remained a 'time capsule' for many years.

Above: The former RAF and ROC Admin building.

With completion of their new 'nuclear proof' operations centre, the staff of No.10 Group ROC took up occupancy in 1960 and remained there for thirty years until, finally, the ROC was 'stood-down' in 1991.

During their existence it is of interest to record the close affinity which the ROC had with the RAF. With similar uniforms, each Group had a parent

RAF station, Poltimore's being RAF St. Mawgan. In addition, the Commandant of the Corps was always a serving RAF Air Commodore.

Above: 10 Group ROC's reinforced concrete bomb-proof Operations Centre.

During subsequent years, apart from the removal of the more valuable equipment, the large operations centre remained virtually untouched. The adjacent buildings became occupied by the Home Office Directorate of Telecommunications and opened as a centre for installing and repairing radio equipment supplied to local police and fire services. They, too, eventually moved out and in 1999 the Home Office put the site up for sale.

Various planning restrictions hampered any early sale of Poltimore but today's visitors will, once more, see the RAF flag fluttering over the site. No, the RAF have not returned, but the site has been taken over by a 'Paint Ball' company which provides 'military style' exploits for the public to enjoy. Whilst the former nuclear-proof operations centre largely remains unchanged, a face-lift to the old administration huts makes them look much more military than they did in the past!

RAF ROBOROUGH (Plymouth)

Plymouth's second RAF station during WWII was near the village of Roborough on the city's north eastern outskirts. The small grass airfield first opened for pleasure flights towards the end of 1923 and was later used by the Plymouth and District Aero Club. Expansion of civil aviation saw the site acquired as the city's Civic Airport in 1931 and it soon played host to a number of the new fledgling airlines. One of the first of these was Great Western Railways which opened a seasonal service to Cardiff in 1932. Later, in 1935, it became the terminus of Provincial Airways' route from London (Croydon) which also made intermediate stops at Southampton and the small Denbury airfield near Newton Abbot. During the same summer a De Havilland Dragon, operated by Railway Air Services, arrived having made a flight from Nottingham via Birmingham, Cardiff and Denbury. Only one of these was to survive to become well known and that was Jersey Airways, an ancestor of FlyBe, today Europe's largest regional airline!

Although a civil airport, from 1935 onwards the RAF occasionally used Roborough for exercises and by a communications flight. In fact in June 1939 it formed No. 15 Group Communications Flight there with a variety of aircraft. However with the outbreak of war all civil passenger flying ceased and the airfield was requisitioned by the Admiralty. Now officially part of HMS Drake, it was used by No. 2 Anti-Aircraft Co-operation Unit for the towing of targets for the nearby gunnery school at Devonport until April 1940 when the unit moved to St. Eval in Cornwall.

By 1940 most of Europe had been overrun by the Nazis and their forces, now massed in France, were facing Britain across the Channel. The Battle of Britain was being fought in our skies and the threat of invasion was a very real one. It was this threat which saw the arrival at Roborough of a flight of

RAF Gloster Gladiators from No.247 Squadron in July 1940, followed by a detachment of Lysanders from No.225 Squadron the following month. Their primary role was to search the coastline of the South West Peninsula for any unusual signs which may be a precursor to the anticipated enemy invasion. The aircraft also had a secondary role, namely air-sea rescue whereby they searched for aircrew shot down over the Channel in order to direct rescue craft to the right location.

Above: A Gloster Gladiator of No.247 Squadron based at Roborough.

The Gladiator was in some respects a remarkable aircraft and the last of the RAF's bi-planes. Although not having entered squadron service until February 1937, this single-seat fighter with its top speed of 250 mph was already obsolete by the outbreak of war. However whilst its role at Roborough was not one destined to bring it into direct contact with enemy Its heroic role during the German siege of Malta ensured its niche in RAF history.

Aware of the shortcomings of the obsolete Gladiators, in early 1941 a detachment of Hurricanes arrived from No.247 Squadron but their stay was only brief for it was soon discovered the airfield's size and lay-out made it difficult for them to operate with the result that they were moved to RAF Portreath, on the north Cornish coast, in May of that year.

Although the RAF had operated from Roborough since the outbreak of war it still technically belonged to the Royal Navy. However in May 1942 it was officially transferred to the RAF. It then came under the control of No.19 Group whose headquarters was at RAF Mount Batten and home to their Communications Flight. However the transfer of 'ownership' made very little difference to activities which, in the main, continued to be confined to the work of the AACU although the change over coincided with the addition of some Fairey Battles and Boulton Paul Defiants, both types having been withdrawn from operational service. Their duties ceased in February 1945. When the war finally ended No.19 Group Communications Flight remained for a while and flew Ansons and Dominies. A gliding school was also opened for the training of Air Training Corps cadets.

The Fairey Battle

Designed as a light bomber, it entered RAF service in May 1937 but soon proved to be under-powered and lacking in any effective defensive firepower. Battle squadrons were quickly decimated by enemy fighters to such an extent they were withdrawn from operational duties and redeployed on training and other duties such as those undertaken at Roborough.

In 1946 the airfield resumed civil flying once more with facilities being run by the local aero club on behalf of the local council. Civil airlines made a return but with the exception of Jersey Airlines all these early ventures were short lived.

However, in 1961 the Royal Navy did make a return with the opening of an Air Experience Flight for the cadets at the Britannia Royal Naval College, Dartmouth, who aspired to become naval aviators. The initial complement of Tiger Moths was replaced by Chipmunks and these remained until the unit closed in the 1990's. Also in the 1960's Sioux helicopters allocated to 41 Commando, Royal Marines, arrived. These were followed by a similar unit from 45 Commando. They remained at Roborough until early 1972 when they re-deployed to new heli-pads at their Coypool base near Plympton. Today this no longer exists, the site being part of the large business park on Plymouth's eastern outskirts.

Roborough's fortunes changed for the better in May 1975 when Brymon Airways obtained the contract for running the airport. With their improvements success followed with numerous new routes introduced, including some to our near neighbours in Normandy and Brittany. This was followed by the building of the airfield's first tarmac runways which allowed aircraft, such as the four-engine Dash-7, to operate from there for the first time. However, further advances in aviation and the inability to cater for the larger jet airliners extensively used by the holiday charter industry and scheduled operators eventually led to the airport's demise. Losing money, its current owners, Sutton Harbour Holdings Ltd., ultimately made the decision that the time had come to cease operations. At the time of going to print Plymouth Airport will cease to exist from the end of 2011.

RAF ROSE DURYARD

Basically included because it is doubted many will have heard of this small RAF Station which comprised a large late Victorian house and grounds in what is today virtually the Exeter University campus. Once home of No.3512 (County of Devon) FCU (Fighter Control Unit), it closed in June 1958. During its years of operation its main task was the training of R.Aux.A.F Fighter Controllers ready for mobilisation should the 'Cold War' escalate into full conflict. Practical experience was gained in co-operation with aircraft from No.3 CAACU based at Exeter Airport and whose role was covered earlier.

No.3512 FCU at RAF Anstruther, Fife, during exercises in 1955

The role of the Fighter Controller was ensure our fighters were in the best position to intercept enemy intruders utilising radar screens indicating such information as aircraft location, direction, height and speed. Local radar stations such as RAF Exminster, with which No.3512 FCU had a close liaison, were extensively reviewed in 'Royal Air Force Air Defence Radar Stations in Devon', by M.J. Passmore. Subsequent to its closure, Rose Duryard was used by a variety of Civil Service Departments but today has been converted to private housing.

RAF UPOTTERY (Smeatharpe)

Situated in the Blackdown Hills of East Devon, and only a few miles from the airfield at Dunkeswell, lies the disused airfield of former RAF Upottery which is more likely to be referred to locally as Smeatharpe after the local hamlet. Today the grass growing up through the disused runways hide the truth about the important role played by this late entrant to WWII. In fact, as we shall see, it seems as if the airfield was built with D-day in mind.

Work on constructing RAF Upottery was not started until the spring of 1943 but, unlike neighbouring Dunkeswell, proceeded on schedule and was completed in time for it to be officially handed over to the RAF in February 1944. This, of course, was just four months before D-day. Initially it was put under the control of No.70 Group and intended to be used as a base for medium bombers such as the B-25 Mitchell and B-26 Marauder operated by the USAAF. However when the Americans arrived in April 1944 their bombers did not come with them. Renaming Upottery as USAAF Station 462, they instead arrived with four squadrons of C-47 Skytrains and its variant the C-53 Skytrooper which formed part of their 439th Troop Carrier Wing. This, in turn, formed part of No.50 Group of the US Troop Carrier Command. Soon afterwards these were joined by Horsa and Waco gliders.

Training was intensified as, by now, the assault on the Normandy beaches was only a matter of weeks away. However, Upottery was not alone in experiencing this flurry of activity. As we read earlier, Exeter was experiencing a similar build-up and, not too far away near Ilminster in Somerset, the airfield at Merryfield was also a hive of American activity together with its near neighbour at Weston Zoyland.

Today a small memorial at Moonhayes Cross, near the disused airfield, gives a good indication of its activity on the 6th June 1944. The memorial, pictured below, is actually incorporated within a red brick sentry box which once used to guard one of the approach roads. The US flag flies from an adjacent pole whilst inside the box itself, shielded by glass, simple wooden crosses recall the names and units of those who, leaving Upottery, were soon to be killed in battle.

The plaque reads:

Upottery - USAAF Station 462

Just after midnight on the 5th June 1944, 81 C-47 unarmed transport aircraft departed from this airfield carrying 1357 Paratroopers who were to be dropped behind enemy lines near the coast of France on D-Day. At dawn on the morning of 7th June, 50 C-47 aircraft towing 30 Horsa gliders and 20 Waco gliders departed for France carrying 958 Glider Infantry Troops in the second wave of the Invasion. Here in honoured memory are those killed on those two missions.

Many years ago the story of D-day formed the background for an epic film, 'The Longest Day', which starred famous British and American actors. In it the role of Colonel Charles Young, who commanded the US paratroopers, was played by the Hollywood legend, John Wayne. What filmgoers probably did not know, however, was that in real life the Colonel and his troops were those leaving Upottery on that memorable night.

Today the revving of engines can occasionally still be heard here for under its local name of Smeatharpe there is now a 'banger' racing stadium on the site. Sometimes, too, you may once again see the airfield alive with US troops and even an old C-47 drop by. The aircraft and the various military vehicles will be real enough but the troops you will see parading around will not. In fact they will be enthusiasts dressing-up for re-enactment weekends arranged by the South West Airfields Heritage Trust.

Above: The Douglas C-47 also known in the RAF as the Dakota.

As well as the runways, one of which features on this book's cover, a few remnants of the former buildings remain on the far side but today these have been incorporated into the local farm.

RAF WESTON ZOYLAND

About four miles south east of Bridgwater, Weston Zoyland was built very close to the site of one of our bloodiest battles, the Battle of Sedgemoor which effectively brought an end to the Monmouth Rebellion, also known as the Pitchfork Rebellion, in 1685. Then rebels fleeing from the scene sought refuge in Weston Zoyland church from where many were taken prisoner and subsequently hanged.

Interestingly it is one of the country's oldest airfields and originates from the 1920's when it was opened as a landing ground to provide aerial facilities for a newly established anti-aircraft gunnery range near Watchet on the North Somerset coast twenty miles away. The first recorded aircraft to use the ground were the Hawker Horsleys of No. 100 Squadron which arrived for a summer camp in the mid 1920's.

A Hawker Horsley

This proved so successful that similar camps were continued. In 1929 the Night Flying Flight arrived from RAF Biggin Hill and it was then renamed the Anti-Aircraft Co-operation Flight.

They continued to operate each summer until 1936 after which it became the home of 'A' Flight, No.1 Anti-Aircraft Co-operation Unit with Wallaces and later Henleys.

With the outbreak of war in September 1939 Weston Zoyland's main task still remained co-operating with the Watchet gunnery range, although two months later a No.16 Squadron detachment of Lysanders arrived for Army Co-operation. These were reinforced the following summer to include coastal patrols in their duties. Increased responsibilities saw a fundamental change at the station when it progressed from a part-time landing ground to a full RAF Station on the 1st September 1940.

For virtually the first three years of the war, Weston Zoyland's role was to provide Army Co-operation although there was a slight change in emphasis between May and December 1942 when No. 239 Squadron re-equipped with Mustangs and took part in operational fighter sweeps before leaving for Andover. However, increasing importance in its primary role and the rapid growth in both aircraft and manpower saw considerable improvements, both in accommodation and an upgrading of the grass runways to tarmac which began in early 1943.

June 1943 saw the formation of the 2nd Tactical Air Force and their aircraft started using Weston Zoyland as a base for air-firing exercises. Then, in September 1943, No.525 Squadron arrived with a derivation of the Wellington, the Warwick, to use for transport duties but, like many other squadrons, their stay was short. They left for Lyneham five months later. This was followed in April 1944 by the departure of other squadrons, mainly to Culmhead and Winkleigh. The airfield was then rapidly prepared for the arrival of the Americans. These were in the form of C-47's and gliders of the 442nd TCG. Shortly afterwards they took part in the Normandy landings.

With the departure of US Forces in the October, Weston Zoyland once more reverted back to its original role as well as hosting a number of fighter squadrons prior to their disbandment. The last squadron to be based there, No.222 equipped with Meteor Mk3's, left in October 1946 and with the local firing ranges now transferred elsewhere the station was placed into Care & Maintenance and virtually abandoned.

However, like its near neighbour Merryfield, resurgence came with the outbreak of the Korean War when it was hurriedly re-opened in June 1952 as No.209 AFS and equipped with Vampires and Meteors. Other changes followed after two years when it briefly became No12 FTS and then home for No.3 All Weather Jet Refresher Squadron.

Now nuclear tests were about to be undertaken in the Pacific and prior to these part of the Atomic Task Force gathered at Weston Zoyland with No.76 Squadron and their Canberras augmented by the Varsity, before leaving for Australia in early Spring 1956. This was not the end of Canberras at the station for Nos. 32 and 73 Squadrons were briefly based there before their eventual deployment to Cyprus in early 1957. Once again reduced to Care & Maintenance it remained Air Ministry property until 1969 when it returned to agricultural use. However, that is not quite the end of the story because part of the old airfield, with the local farmer's permission, later became a home for hang-glider enthusiasts.

Canberra 1956   Microlite 2005

RAF WINKLEIGH

Today the A3124 road, which links the A30 at Whiddon Down with North Devon at Torrington, cuts right through this WWII airfield where construction started in 1940 as a satellite for RAF Chivenor. It was one of the few areas of level ground around but on laying its runways they encountered a major problem - the ground was 'boggy', making it difficult for the foundations to stabilise. In fact it was not until the end of 1941 that it underwent its first inspection and that was a test it failed. A further twelve months passed but by then Coastal Command, whose aircraft operated from Chivenor, decided they no longer wanted it.

On 1st January 1943 it was placed under the control of Fighter Command. Eye witness reports say it was 'a mess'. There was mud everywhere, the runways were below the level of the road and there was still no accommodation. Still trying to get the airfield operational, the contractors did manage to erect one hanger and eight Blisters together with a standard control tower on some higher ground. During February and March the manpower moved onto the camp from temporary billets in Winkleigh village and records show the first aircraft landed on the 24th April. However, by now nobody had any real idea what to do with it and so on the 20th August, 1943, it s status was reduced to Care & Maintenance.

Just when Winkleigh seemed doomed as an operational airfield things suddenly perked up when in October 1943 it was reopened for the USAAF. Initially there requirement was as a base for pre-invasion exercises when their troops made practice landings on the wide North Devon beaches. Spitfires flown by American pilots of the 12th Recce Squadron, IXth Fighter

Command, USAAF, arrived to provide tactical reconnaissance whilst the training took place. They remained until the end of the year but other US aircraft were continually arriving, in the main C-47s ferrying US troops.

Until now, whilst a hive of activity, there was no permanent squadron based at the airfield. This was rectified in April in April 1944 when No.406 (RCAF) Squadron arrived from Exeter with their Beaufighters and were soon in action, shooting down a Ju88 off Start Point on the 23rd of the month. Also arriving were a number of Mosquito XII's and on their first night of action, on April 29th, one of their aircraft shot down two Dornier 217's in the space of eleven minutes.

Above: The Albacore. Designed as a 3-crew replacement for the Swordfish

As D-day drew near a detachment of Hurricanes and Defiants from No.286 Squadron arrived and these were joined in early May by another Canadian squadron, No.415, with their Albacores. Their main role was night patrols to prevent German E-boats penetrating our training areas along the south coast. This had in fact occurred in April 1944 off Slapton Sands in South Devon when enemy E-boats penetrated 'Operation Eagle', destroying many landing craft and killing over seven hundred US troops. It was an event of which the full details were not disclosed by the Pentagon until 1994.

Routine patrols continued throughout early June and Winkleigh based aircraft continued their successes with their Mosquitoes undertaking intruder missions over France, attacking targets of choice which included enemy transport , including trains and military convoys, and airports. By now, also operating from the airfield were Lysanders of No.161 Squadron who flew clandestine missions into occupied France where they picked up Allied agents and left replacements.

On the 16th September 1944, No.415 Squadron left and the airfield was temporarily placed on Care & Maintenance status. This proved to be short lived for in the November it was transferred to No.23 Group to become a training station for the recruits who would become the backbone of a newly reformed Royal Norwegian Air Force. An initial establishment of twelve Harvards arrived and these were augmented by a number of Cornells which came over from training bases in Canada. Training continued until November 1945 when forty-four aircraft and their Norwegian airmen returned to home soil near Oslo.

With the departure of the Norwegians no further flying took place at Winkleigh although the airfield remained under the control of No.23 Group until the end of June 1948. It then transferred from the Air Ministry to the Ministry of Agriculture and Fisheries although in October 1956 they took back control again. It then became an intended satellite of Chivenor but in reality it was never used and after two years the Air Ministry disposed of it yet again.

Today, with the main road passing through it, a number of vestiges can still be seen. Whilst the area is now a sprawling industrial site, and seemingly littered with numerous large vehicles, the old control tower can be plainly seen from the road although now in quite a poor state of preservation. Faring slightly better, on the south side of the road and incorporated into an industrial complex, are a number of the former station buildings. Although now on private land, many can be seen from the public road.

Above: The former RAF Winkleigh control tower and one of the station's buildings. Both can be seen without entering private land.

Personal Recollections of Those who Served

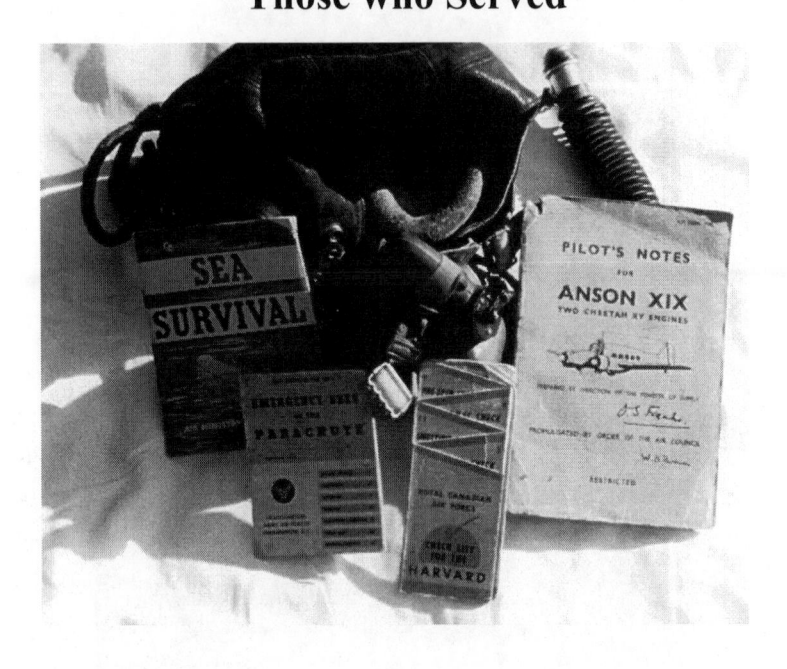

' When once you have tasted flight, you will forever walk the earth with your eyes turned skyward, for there you have been, and there you will always long to return'

Leonardo da Vinci   1452-1519

A Test Pilot's Life.

Graham ANDREWS

Graham was born in Birmingham on 28th May 1937 and was educated at King Edward's School where he was a member of the school's Combined Cadet Force and one of a select few to win an RAF Flying Scholarship. With this award he learned to fly on Tiger Moths at the Coventry Aero Club and had gained a Private Pilots Licence before he reached the age of 18. A cadetship at the RAF College Cranwell followed, training as a pilot on the piston engine Provost and the jet engine Vampire.

The Provost   The Vampire T11

It was whilst at Cranwell that Graham became one of the few who have, by necessity, ejected from an aircraft in flight. This occurred in December 1957 whilst practicing high level aerobatics at 25,000 feet in a Vampire T11. He was in the middle of a slow roll when the rudder cable snapped. The aircraft immediately went into a high-rotational spin and became uncontrollable with severe vibration. After falling to 15,000 feet he and his instructor ejected.

After graduating from Cranwell he attended 231 OCU, RAF Bassingbourn, to train on the photo reconnaissance Canberra. Completion of the conversion course saw Graham posted to Germany in February 1959 where he joined No.31 Squadron at RAF Laarbruch which flew the photo reconnaissance version of the Canberra Mk.7. This had an exceptionally high ceiling, said to be in excess of 50,000 feet, and coupled with a range in excess of 6000 kms, its advanced photographic equipment made it an ideal aircraft for the role in which it was deployed. Much of its operational work remains 'classified' but it is safe to say that during the 'Cold War' it was keeping a very close eye on any potential threats from perceived hostile countries.

Graham's tour with 31 Squadron ended in August 1961 when he returned to the UK and trained as an instructor (QFI) at the Central Flying School, Little Rissington, qualifying as 'top of class'. The result of his high marks was a return to the RAF College at Cranwell as a QFI, the only difference now being that the new basic trainer was the Jet Provost. This was a three year tour at the end of which came a new posting setting the scene for the rest of his long career in aviation.

In February 1965 he arrived at the Empire Test Pilots School at Boscombe Down to qualify as a test pilot and was initially chosen to be the Project Pilot (designate) for the new TSR 2 aircraft which was to be a world beater. Sadly, as is so often the case, a change of heart by the Government saw the cancellation of this prestigious project in the autumn, soon after his arrival. Nevertheless, there was no let-up in his new role as a test pilot for, moving to the Aircraft and Armament Experimental Establishment (A & AEE) at the same station, he became Project Pilot on the Lightning Mk6 and also for the Phantom and Jaguar. In addition he was involved in trials with numerous other aircraft including the Javelin and Harrier. Larger 4-engine aircraft included the Shackleton and the Belfast.

It was whilst at Boscombe Down he was promoted to Squadron Leader and also awarded the *'Queen's Commendation for Valuable Service in the Air'* for his work as a test pilot.

In December 1968 he joined Test Flight Operations at the Royal Aeronautical Establishment (RAE) at Farnborough but in October the following year he made a far reaching decision to retire early for reasons he states were *"in the National interest"*.

It could be argued that his reason was a valid one for he had been offered the post of becoming a test pilot for Rolls-Royce. This was an era when Rolls-Royce, whose engines were already rated the best in the world, were pushing new frontiers in terms of power and efficiency and the role for Graham was to test fly all aircraft to be fitted with their engines during the development stage. For the first eighteen months he was based at their Test Flight Establishment, Hucknall, where one the many aircraft he flew was the VC-10 which was being used as a test bed for the new RB211 engine.

Pictured above are two of the aircraft types flown by Graham whilst at Filton. Left is the VC-10 and, on the right, the Avro Vulcan.

Between 1971 and 1981 his office was at their Filton factory and airfield near Bristol. Here the first six years were extremely busy and included tests with the Vulcan which was being used as a test bed for the RB199 engine. However, it was not only fixed wing aircraft being tested for his duties also involved test flying helicopters, including the Scout, Lynx and Sea King. In 1973 he had become the deputy Chief Test Pilot and three years later became Chief Test Pilot and Chief of Flight Operations.

To the average reader, however, perhaps the pinnacle of his test flying career came when appointed to chair the Engine Handling Panel for, arguably, Britain's most prestigious aircraft, Concorde. This meant Graham flying it on a number of occasions but one story, of which there has been little publicity, concerned fears of the public's conception of supersonic flight and its sonic boom, particularly if heard over a heavily populated area such as London. To gauge public reaction prior to Concorde's maiden flight a number of tests were carried out at various occasions which involved flying a Lightning through the sound barrier. Graham was involved in a number of these but his account of the tests over London is particularly interesting, as he now relates:

"Actually the first proposed test over London was postponed when it was discovered it would coincide with a Royal Garden Party at the Palace and the last thing we wanted was to rattle the Queen's tea cups! It was postponed until the following Tuesday when I was scheduled to carry it out. I would be flying at 1.4 mach at 43,000 feet which would create the same effect as Concorde breaking the sound barrier at Mach 2 at 60,000 feet. I also timed my run so that the sonic boom would occur at the same time as Big Ben struck the hour! The public had been forewarned so we were expecting some complaints but in actual fact only two were officially upheld.

The most serious of these was from an eye surgeon who said that had it occurred a few minutes earlier it may have affected his concentration whilst undertaking delicate eye surgery. The second related to some of the patients at a mental institution becoming disturbed. However that is not quite the end of the story for that day's edition of the London evening paper carried the headline 'Avengers over London'. Somehow they had obtained the names of those engaged in the project and one of the other pilots was Hugh Rigg, the brother of Diana Rigg who was, of course, the popular star of the T.V. series 'The Avengers'. The only problem was he was not flying the aircraft, I was!"

Sadly, by the latter half of the 1970's Britain's aircraft industry was going into decline due to increased competition, in particular from the USA. The RAF was also contracting in size. New projects for Rolls-Royce were declining and Graham was asked to make significant staff cuts in his department. An alternative suggestion of his was rejected and, as the proposed redundancy terms were generous, Graham decided to also avail himself of them, retiring from the company in October 1981.

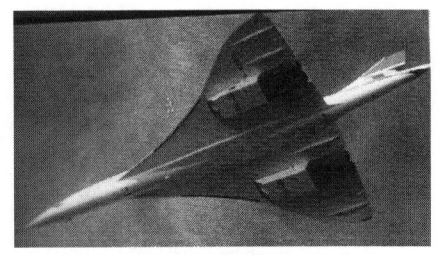

Above: (left) The English Electric Lightning and (right) Concorde.

Initially he thought of a career in education by becoming a mathematics and physics teacher, two subjects where he had valuable in-depth experience. He was accepted for a teacher training course through Bristol University but the Department of Education stepped in, saying that without a 'first degree', he would be unable to teach in a state school. Beaten by bureaucracy, he decided to remain in civil aviation, flying freelance. This was to lead to one of the greatest changes imaginable.

From being involved with the development and flying of Concorde, for two years between 1982 and 1984 he became involved with microlight flying, becoming Chairman of the British Microlight Aircraft Association and their only qualified test pilot. During his period of Chairmanship he also drew up operating standards for the aircraft which were agreed by the Civil Aviation Authority but somewhat floundered during the increasing long implementation process. Thus thwarted, he decided to return to mainstream aviation again.

This opportunity arose in April 1985 when he joined Shorts of Belfast as the second experimental test pilot. The following year he became their Deputy Chief Test Pilot and in 1990 their Chief Test Pilot. Initially this was a very busy period for Shorts had been awarded the contract for the RAF's new basic trainer, the Tucano.

The Shorts Tucano.

Another main project of his was the Super Sherpa, a light troop and freight carrying aircraft based on the Short 360, and destined for the US Forces as the C23B. However, first considerable trials had to be carried out in an environment chosen by them which turned out to be a rudimentary airstrip in Alaska! Graham duly made the flight and obliged!

Another change in Graham's career came in 1990 when Bombardier of Canada took over Shorts, cancelled all their future projects and relegated the company to a parts supplier. As a result he joined the Civil Aviation Authority as a Flight Examiner, undertaking work for them until 1998 when he moved to Exmouth to become Chief Training Captain for Jersey European Airways, the HQ for which was at Exeter International Airport. The company has since vastly expanded and is now FlyBe, Europe's largest regional airline.

On reaching his 65th birthday in 2002 Graham had to retire from an active flying role within the public transport industry but was able to continue as a Consultant. Amongst those still seeking his advice are FlyBe and, occasionally, Shorts. Few, like Graham, can say they have fifty years flying experience and in that time he has flown a record breaking 177 different types of aircraft, amassed over 13,000 flying hours mostly on test flights of short duration, and has over 1000 hours of flying on helicopters.

Today he and his wife, Nathalie, enjoy a semi-retirement in Exmouth where he is a valuable member of the local Aircrew Association.

THIRTY SIX COLLEAGUES LOST IN ONE RAID

F.C. BLACKMORE MBE

'Blackie', as he prefers to be known, was born in Exeter in July 1923, his parents living in a tied cottage owned by the Rector of a Devon village. When the Rector died they moved to Honiton and the nearby village of Offwell from where he attended Honiton Secondary Modern School. On completing his education he became a baker and confectioner.

However, he had already developed an interest in flying and had joined the local Air Training Corps. This stood him in good stead for he was accepted for Aircrew and was called up in July 1942. This began with being kitted out at RAF Padgate and then moving to an ITW at the Victoria Hotel, Filey, for 'square bashing' (drill). He says it was quite eerie at night doing guard duty, standing staring out to sea with a Lee Enfield rifle and no ammunition whilst thinking the Germans were just the other side of the North Sea!

His aircrew training began in earnest when four weeks later he was posted to RAF St. Athan in South Wales to complete a three month Flight Mechanics course. Then it was off to Squires Gate, Blackpool where he was billeted in private holiday accommodation at South Shore whilst completing a Fitters course. With that, too, successfully completed it was a return to St. Athan to undertake a Flight Engineers course. Blackie makes the observation that later in the war this rather protracted procedure was condensed to just one Flight Engineers course at St. Athan. With his training successfully completed he was promoted to Sergeant and posted to No.1658 Heavy Conversion Unit at Riccall in Yorkshire. It was here he joined up with the rest of his crew to gain experience on the Halifax bomber before being posted to a newly formed Squadron, No.578, at RAF Burn, just South of Selby in Yorkshire. Shortly after his arrival the squadron converted to the later version of the Halifax, the Mk.3, with Bristol Hercules engines.

Blackie flew his first operational sortie on the 19th February 1944 which entailed a 7hour 20 minute flight to bomb targets in Stuttgart and was described by him as 'uneventful'. A further six 'ops' were flown to targets such as Le Mans, Stuttgart, Augsburg and Frankfurt during which the squadron lost six of their aircraft before, on the 24th March 1944, Blackie took off on his longest raid so far ... to Berlin. He describes that flight:

"It was quite an exciting night although, unfortunately, we did not reach our target. Our aircraft, LK X, was fitted with an experimental wing bomb bay overload petrol tanks instead of the usual ones which were normally fitted to the main bomb bays. Our route was across the North Sea, then Denmark, across the Baltic and then a starboard turn for the final run to the target, Berlin. Whilst flying over Denmark it was my job to begin pumping the fuel from the overload tanks into the main ones but it soon became obvious that, although the overload gauges were dropping, the ones for the main tanks were not rising! The only reason which seemed feasible was that somehow the fuel was being pumped out into the atmosphere. We continued with the pumping when, following discussion with the navigator and myself, the pilot realised that if we continued to Berlin we would not have enough fuel to return home but crash somewhere in the Low Countries. With little real option it was decided to abort the mission but rather than waste our bomb load we also decided to attack Kiel from 20,000 feet on the way home. This we did but encountered such heavy flak that we dived to

only 2,000 feet to avoid it before making for home across the North Sea. A subsequent investigation showed that the two valves in the new fuel lines to the wing bomb bay overload tanks had been fitted incorrectly. On a more personal note, although we carried out an attack on Kiel, because we did not reach our target of Berlin the Air Ministry would not allow us to count the flight towards our total required to complete a full tour of operations."

Blackie has kept a copy of the squadron records for all of his flights and one concerning a raid on Bottrop, near Essen, on the night of 20/21st July 1944 is reproduced here. It reads:

"26 aircraft away between 22.26 and 23.24 hours on the 20th and of these six were lost. Two abandoned the operation and 18 bombed the primary target LK Q abandoned with port inner engine unserviceable and LK Z with instrument failure. LK E and LK K collided in the Hull area and all 14 crew were killed. I witnessed this crash whilst looking out of our astrodome.

        LK D was posted as missing - no survivors
        LK M was posted as missing - two survivors
        LK P was posted as missing - four survivors
        LK C was posted as missing - no survivors.

Weather was good over the target area. Flak defences in barrage form were used 16,000 to 21,000 feet and many ineffectual searchlights were seen. Operation was thought to be a success and well concentrated considering the opposition. LK T suffered a fire in its starboard engine."

With each Halifax carrying a crew of seven it is worth recording that during this one raid 36 aircrew, all Blackie's colleagues from one squadron, No.578, lost their lives.

Blackie flew a number of 'ops' to other targets in the Ruhr and was one of the fortunate ones to survive and complete a full tour of 36 operations over occupied Europe. On the 26th October 1944 he was posted to RAF Leconfield to join Transport Command's No.96 Squadron. He was also on stand-by to transfer to the Far East to participate in the war against the Japanese although, he says, thankfully the two Atom bombs dropped on Hiroshima and Nagasaki meant this did not materialise. This sudden end to the war saw him moving back to the West Country, this time to RAF St. Mawgan to assist with the installation of a new approach system. He remained there until he was demobilised on the 8th October 1946.

He returned to his pre-war occupation of baker and confectioner until five years later he joined the Home Office to work at their new Supply and Transport Store being opened at former RAF Dunkeswell, near Honiton. This was the beginning of a long career within the Home Office which saw him moving to many sites within the UK and with various promotions which eventually saw him becoming the Superintendent of all Supply and Transport Stores. It was a career which saw him rewarded with the MBE when he retired at the age of 60 in 1983. He says that meeting the Queen, with his wife Betty, whom he had courted since school days, was one of the happiest of his life. Betty died in 1964 after a long illness but eventually Blackie found happiness again. Sadly, however, Pam his wife for almost the past 25 years, passed away whilst this book was being compiled.

Today, a member of the East Devon Aircrew Association, he lives in Honiton and has been active in many local organisations including Feniton Bowling Club and as a church warden.

' One for PHILATELISTS! '

Robert M. BURNS

It is extremely doubtful that the well-known Scottish poet led such an interesting life as his namesake who served some twenty-seven years in the British Army. 'Bob' Burns, as he prefers to be called, is by birth a 'Man of Kent' having been born in Gillingham in August 1947. Completing his education in the local Secondary Modern School, he knew exactly what he wanted to do on leaving. In 1962, at the age of sixteen, he immediately enlisted as a 'boy soldier' and came to Devon for the first time to start training with the Junior Leaders Regiment at Denbury, near Newton Abbot. Initially set for a career in the Corps of Royal Signals, the following year a change of career options saw him moving to the All Arms Junior Leaders Regiment at Towyn in North Wales from where he joined the Corps of Royal Military Police and was posted to Germany in 1966.

Asked about his time in Germany he said it was no more than routine ... but he did get involved with a murder trial when soldier's wife murdered her husband! However having now completed five years in the army, Bob went through a phase facing many servicemen, whether to stay or leave. He decided to leave but, realising how much he missed service life, within twelve months had re-enlisted although not to return to the Military Police.

Initially he joined the 3rd Royal Tank Regiment where he became a driver / operator on the Regiment's armoured cars but when a posting to Germany came through this was to join No.9 Flight of the Army Air Corps as the second crew member of the small Sioux helicopter.

Returning from Germany in 1972 Bob's career was to take another twist when he saw a future in the Army Air Corps. Now a Corporal, he undertook an Air Gunners' Course at AAC Middle Wallop which, interestingly, saw his name receive international recognition. This came about when in July 1973 the camp was chosen as the location for the 'World Helicopter Championships'. A special First Day cover was designed for the occasion and, for authenticity, these were all flown in Army Air Corps Gazelle XW847.

The First Day Cover … postage was 3d!

The aircraft itself was significant because XW847 was the first Gazelle to enter British Army service when it was accepted three months earlier, on the 27th April. The front of the Special First Day Covers, in addition to the aircraft details, also listed the helicopter crew making this historic flight and there, below the name of the pilot, Captain B.A. Horsey DFM AAC, appears the name of Cpl. R.M. Burns RTR. as the aircraft's Flight Recorder.

Course completed, Bob became a member of the Army Air Corp's 664 Parachute Squadron, part of the 16 Parachute Brigade based at Farnborough. Undertaking numerous training and tactical exercises, he remained here until 1976 when he returned to Germany again. Now a Sergeant, he joined No.653 Squadron, which operated the Scout helicopter, with the specific role of Assistant Helicopter Weapons Instructor. Asked about their role in Germany he would only say:

"It was all very routine. Of course it was still a divided country and there was always the perceived threat of military action from the East against which we were kept in constant readiness. Our role was to provide support for the ground troops should any problem arise. However keeping ready was not without its moments and I spent three detachments in Canada where we used their ranges in Alberta for practising our missile firing. Then there was a period spent on a Mountain Rescue Course at Aviemore in Scotland when, in particular, we were testing out 'long drop' techniques which meant lowering a rope over 200 feet onto a precise spot."

Further promotion, this time to Staff Sergeant, came in 1978 when he left Germany to return to the UK as an Instructor at the Junior Leaders Regiment based at Bovington. This covered many subjects essential to the training of future NCOs. However when the tour ended in 1981 it was back to Germany once more but not before undertaking a conversion course onto the Lynx and being promoted to Warrant Officer 2. His new squadron in Germany was No.651 which operated the Lynx whilst his own particular role was that of Helicopter Weapons Instructor. Although this was a three year tour, from 1981 - 1984, it seems that Bob spent more time away from Germany than actually there for the Squadron always seemed to be deployed elsewhere. Asking him to explain, he replied:

"Well we served a number of detachments in Northern Ireland where, of course, at that time our Forces were very much engaged against the IRA. Our role came in many forms but basically it was always in support of the troops on the ground. This could come in various ways, from providing air cover during tactical operations to ferrying troops, or supplies, quickly and safely from one point of need to another. However our longest engagement came in 1983 when we were detached to the Falklands and were the first Lynx Squadron to be deployed there. Again our role was purely in support of the ground troops. The terrain and conditions were such that the only way any supplies could reach them was by air and that's where we came in. Basically it was a logistics operation. "

After his return from the Falklands, between 1984 and 1987 he was back at Middle Wallop, not only as an Instructor at the AAC Aircrew Training Squadron but also as the Regimental Sergeant Major. His vast knowledge of helicopter weaponry was to keep him in this field for the rest of his service with his last posting to Netheravon. Here, as the Theatre Helicopter Weapons Instructor, he had a responsibility for all weapons training and trapping world-wide, with the exception of Germany. Asked if there were any particular incidents, such as dangerous moments, he could now recall he replied, rather laconically:

"Not really but I suppose given the jobs we often had to do there's always an element of danger flying. In fact during the six months I was the RSM at Middle Wallop I attended five funerals, one being the RSM I was standing in for. When a newcomer joined the Mess the others used to tell them not to

get too friendly with me or I'd end up burying them! However, it was not all gloom and doom because another memory is of acting as an instructor to the young Prince Edward. He was undergoing training as a Royal Marine Officer at the time and came to Middle Wallop on a short instructional course and I was the one who took him through the weapon systems on the Lynx helicopter."

Above: Bob in the Falklands beside the wreckage of an Argentine Air Force Pucara which had been shot down.

With almost 2000 flying hours on helicopters, Bob retired from the Army Air Corps in October 1987 but did not completely sever all links with the Army for, becoming a civil servant, he had a particular role in the management of service accommodation. When final retirement came a love of the sea brought him and his wife, Caroline, to Exmouth. As well as being a member of the East Devon Aircrew Association he is very active with the National Coast Watch Institution and is currently manager of the Exmouth station.

FROM FLYING BOATS TO FLYING JETS

Cyril Beaumont CLEVERLY

Cyril was born in Dover in April 1920 and educated at the local Grammar School. Always interested in mechanics he opted for employment as an auto mechanic on leaving school, a move which was to set him on an interesting future career after he joined the RAF on the 22nd December 1940. On enlisting at RAF Cardington Cyril's civilian qualifications saw him classified as a Direct Entry Fitter 2 which, following a six month course at Hedresford, was upgraded to Fitter 1 (Engines). His first posting to an operational unit followed in June 1941 when he joined the AACU (Anti-aircraft Co-operation Unit) at Gosport which operated a variety of aircraft such as the Gloster Gladiator, Hawker Henley and Fairey Battle.

Cyril recalls that his first job after arriving was to change the engine on one of the Fairey Battles, replacing an early model Merlin Mk1 engine with a newer Mk 3. It was in this Battle he had his first flight when it was taken up for its subsequent air test. Some ironically say that fitters were made to accompany the pilot on such tests just to ensure they did a good job! However, it was whilst at Gosport Cyril learned that the new era of four-engine bombers flew with a Flight Engineer as a member of crew and the idea appealed to him. He spoke to his Warrant Officer, an engineer with many years pre-war service, who thought he was mad but nevertheless recommended him for further training as such. With this recommendation Cyril's next move was to RAF St. Athan in South Wales to undertake the requisite course.

He describes his arrival as follows:

"There were dozens of us there waiting for the next courses for Lancasters, Halifaxes and Stirlings. Then they mentioned another extra course for the Sunderland flying boat. As most of them seemed to want to go on the Lancaster course I opted for the Sunderland and was accepted. After a two week short course at St. Athan I was off to Short Bros at Rochester to see them being built. A return to St. Athan followed for the results of my tests, all was well and I was promoted to Sergeant in October 1942."

However, it was not quite the end of Cyril's training for the Flight Engineer on the Sunderland also had to be prepared to act as an Air Gunner, a requisite which saw him undertaking a course at No.10 Air Gunnery School, Barrow, with live firing from the upper gun turret of a Defiant. He passed with a score assessed as being above average. Now categorised as a Flight Engineer/Air Gunner he was sent north to Invergordon for crew training. Cyril succinctly said what happened next:

"Typical of the RAF I was not put on Sunderlands but Catalinas, an aircraft I had never seen before! I did some flying then, in early January 1943, twenty of us were told we had to go to Handley Page, Liverpool, for a full course on the Handley Page Halifax Mk.2. Three weeks in the classroom followed, then off to Derby for a course on the Rolls-Royce Merlin 20 engines by which time we were wondering where it was all leading."

The answer was that two special squadrons were being formed for use by Coastal Command using extra long-range Halifaxes capable of taking the hunt for enemy U-boats even further out into the Atlantic. Cyril was to join one of these squadrons, No.502, and duly arrived at RAF St. Eval on the North Cornwall coast to meet his new crew and undertake familiarisation.

However, with that completed, they were moved to Holmsley South, in the New Forest just North of Bournemouth. It was from here, on the 1st April 1943, that Cyril made his first operational flight, searching for U-boats ahead of a large convoy. Other such flights took place but one in particular, at the end of April, stayed in Cyril's memory and perhaps illustrates the value of having an engineer on board. He describes what happened:

" The electric booster pump in no.1 tank of the 4 we had in fuselage bomb bay failed, each of the tanks holding over 200 gallons. Without the fuel we would be unable to carry on and without our presence the convoy could be threatened. I suggested I could make a jury pipe, fitting one end to the main fuel line and the other in the bomb bay fuel tank so that the engine fuel pump could draw up the petrol. It was something I'd learned at Rolls-Royce in Derby and it worked. I then did the same with the other inner engine and that worked too. The result was we were able to carry on protecting the convoy and although we didn't see any U-boats I like to think it was our presence which prevented any attack. Some months later I learned I had been 'Mentioned in Despatches'."

In September 1943 the Squadron moved to St. Davids in Wales. Two months later their first pilot, with his tour completed, went on rest leave and their second pilot, a South African, took over in his place. That month they flew another ten anti-submarine patrols, averaging ten hours duration each, and Cyril was promoted to Flight Sergeant. The following month, December, the squadron were put on 'shipping strike', i.e. seek and destroy enemy shipping. Their first encounter came on the 28th December 1943 when an enemy vessel was sighted making for a French port. A Liberator from another squadron was the first to sight the vessel but although managing to set it on fire they failed to sink it. When Cyril's aircraft arrived their orders were to 'bomb and sink'. However, it was not all plain sailing for on the way to the encounter one Halifax was lost without trace, all were friends of Cyril.

Although subsequently air-sea rescue patrols were sent out only one dinghy was found and that, ironically, contained two Germans. However, the mission was successful as Cyril's photograph shows.

The night of 29th January 1944 was another date that Cyril recalls vividly:

" We were well out over the Atlantic when our 'radar op' obtained a good sighting about ten miles away so we went to 'action stations' and when we were about three miles from the potential target we dropped several delayed action flares. When these lit up there, in the centre of the flare path, was a U-boat on the surface. We commenced an attack at 1000 ft having been warned that if we went any lower the blast from our huge depth bombs could blow our tail off! As we came in it was "steady, steady, left, steady hold, bombs gone". We had dropped all three of our special bombs with 600lbs of 'Torpex' in each. A few moments later there were three 'thrumps'! Having the astro-dome above my Flight Engineer's station I had an excellent view. The first bomb fell on the starboard side, the second on the port and the third a little ahead. Three columns of water with the U-boat in the middle looking bent. I watched the sea subside whilst the U- boat fell

back and broke in two. Each part began to sink and then she was gone. There were no survivors."

In the March the Squadron was switched to anti E-boat patrols which Cyril describes as more routine than exciting although on one occasion they made radar contact with six heading down the Channel. These were subsequently intercepted by two Royal Navy destroyers which sunk two and damaged three with only one escaping unscathed. However, by May he had completed his 50 sorties and was due for a rest and some leave. On his return he was posted to a Halifax Heavy Conversion Unit as an instructor and later promoted to Warrant Officer.

Cyril's story might have ended there but for the fact that as the war drew to a close there was a demand for RAF aircrew to be seconded to civil aviation to assist in its post-war recovery. Cyril responded to an appeal by BOAC and was accepted, starting his secondment in September 1945. In June 1946 he was demobilised from the RAF and BOAC offered him a permanent position as a Flight Engineer. He was soon flying the world on Sunderland, Constellation, and Boeing Stratocruiser aircraft before converting to new jet airliners such as the Boeing 707 and the De Havilland Comet.

He retired on his 55th birthday and lived with his wife Mavis, whom he married in March 1945, in the East Devon village of Colyford. A keen supporter of the Aircrew Association, Cyril sadly died in July 2011, shortly after providing the material for this book. He was ninety-one.

A COLD BATH IN A NORWEGIAN LAKE!

Ronald F. DAY

Born on Christmas Day, 1922, in Taunton, Ron was educated locally at Taunton School and on leaving initially found employment as a junior clerk with the local council. At the age of nineteen he volunteered for aircrew duties and, having been assessed as a potential Observer, two months after his twentieth birthday he reported to the Aircrew Reception Centre (ACRC) at Regents Park in London. With all recruitment procedures completed, it was then a return to the West Country with a posting to an Initial Training Wing (ITW) at Babbacombe. He recalls that whilst there his Flight had to give a PT presentation to a visiting member of the royal family and how training for this meant he eventually left Babbacombe fitter than he had ever been before ... or since !

Completing ITW saw Ron's next move to No.1 Signal School, Cranwell, for a fourteen week course towards eventually becoming a Nav/W, I.e. a combination of both navigator and wireless operator. Inevitably this meant you were destined for 2-crew aircraft. However, that was still for the future. In the meanwhile training at Cranwell included flights in a de Havilland Rapide, on one occasion 14 flights being made in one week. Then, with this aspect of training completed, Ron found himself on the 'RMS Queen Elizabeth' and one week later disembarking in New York. An overland journey followed which saw him crossing the border into Canada to attend No.33 Air Navigation School, at RCAF Mount Hope, Hamilton, Ontario. Whilst there Ron's sixteen week course was extended after an outbreak of scarlet fever hit the camp and he became one of its victims.

Fortunately he succumbed towards the end of the course and, whilst lying in his hospital bed, learned he had passed and received his navigator's brevet. There was also a bright side and Ron recalls that following a mandatory three week stay in hospital he was entitled to 10 days sick leave. With memories of their glimpse of New York on arrival he and two other convalescing mates wasted no time in heading back to the 'Big Apple' where they enjoyed eight 'never to be forgotten' days.

Still more training lay ahead and from Mount Hope it was to RCAF Charlotte Town on Prince Edward Island for a six week General Reconnaissance Course utilising the ubiquitous Anson. By now it was the summer of 1943 and with training in Canada completed it was back to New York again to board the 'Aquitania' for the return voyage to the UK, this time sleeping in a bunk in the open on Promenade Deck.

October 1943 was spent on further general reconnaissance training before, in December, being posted to join No.455 Squadron RAAF based at RAF Leuchars in Scotland and at the time converting from the Hampden to the Beaufighter. It was just before Christmas when Ron had his first flight in the latter and the next three months saw the squadron 'working up' on the new aircraft ready for their first operations. With this phase completed, the squadron moved to Langham, on the Norfolk coast, where in April 1943 they teamed up with No.489 Squadron of the RNZAF and commenced operations the same month. Armament on their 445 Squadron aircraft comprised 8 rockets and 4X20mm cannon which were used to silence escorting flak ships 'sperrbreshers' with the object of providing No.489 Squadron, with their torpedoes, as clear a run as possible. Together with squadrons based at Northcoates in Lincolnshire the combined units were known as Strike Wings. These operated throughout the summer of 1944, looking for German shipping along the Friesian Islands or Southern Norway or for E-boats operating in the English Channel.

Above: A rocket firing Beaufighter used by the Strike Wings.

It was during this period that Ron was commissioned and in October he and his squadron, together with No.489, moved from Norfolk to Dallachy on the Moray Firth in Scotland, a location from which they were better able to attack enemy shipping operating off Norway and also in the fjords.   He remained here until the following April when he was posted a few miles further East, to Banff, to join No. 235 Squadron which operated as part of the Mosquito Strike Force, Ron making his first flight in the Mosquito on the 6th April 1945. Ironically it was almost his last, that coming a few days later on the 11th April, a day he is unlikely to ever forget.

He recalls that day vividly: *"We were part of a group of some 40 aircraft briefed to attack enemy shipping in the Southern Norwegian port of Porsgrunn which, I guess, proved to be our defining moment. Having made the attack we aimed to get away from the area as quickly as possible but Phil Davenport, my Australian pilot, was having problems with the aircraft's controls.   It was then I saw coolant streaming out of the starboard engine and realised we had been hit.   By now we were very low over the tree tops of a pine forest with a lake largely covered in ice just ahead.*

Phil, an excellent pilot, realised this was our only chance of possible survival and indicated to me that we were going to ditch. I immediately jettisoned the top hatch but on later reflection do not think I had time to re-fasten my harness again before the impact of hitting the water. Somehow we got out of the aircraft and managed to scramble out of the freezing cold water into our dinghy which had self inflated. However, during the impact of landing I had received a blow on the head and lapsed into unconsciousness. As a result it was only later that I learned that four Norwegian farmers had heroically launched a small boat and rowed through broken ice to rescue us. Then, having brought us ashore lit a fire and fetched blankets to save us from hypothermia. Undoubtedly they saved our lives. Unfortunately they were not the only ones to witness our crash and German troops arrived before the Norwegian underground could spirit us away. The next day we were taken to Oslo where Phil was placed in a make-shift cell on Gardemoen Airfield but because I was diagnosed by a doctor as having severe concussion I was taken to hospital where I was well treated and languished until the 10th May. Then, suddenly, overnight everything changed. I was told I was free and that Oslo was now under control of the Norwegian Resistance and the Germans were 'Kaput'!

Ron's repatriation home was in a Stirling bomber which had been converted to carry troops of the Airborne Division to Norway and he describes his RAF career thereafter as 'rather mundane'.

After attending an Intelligence Course, he became an Intelligence Officer at RAF Chivenor. However, with hostilities over, this amounted to briefing crews of Halifax bombers then employed on meteorological night flights. He remained at Chivenor until June 1946 when he was demobilised through Mount Wise in Plymouth.

Above: A Mosquito Mk VI of Strike Wing similar to that in which Ron was shot down. Below: A map of the target, the harbour at Porsgrunn.

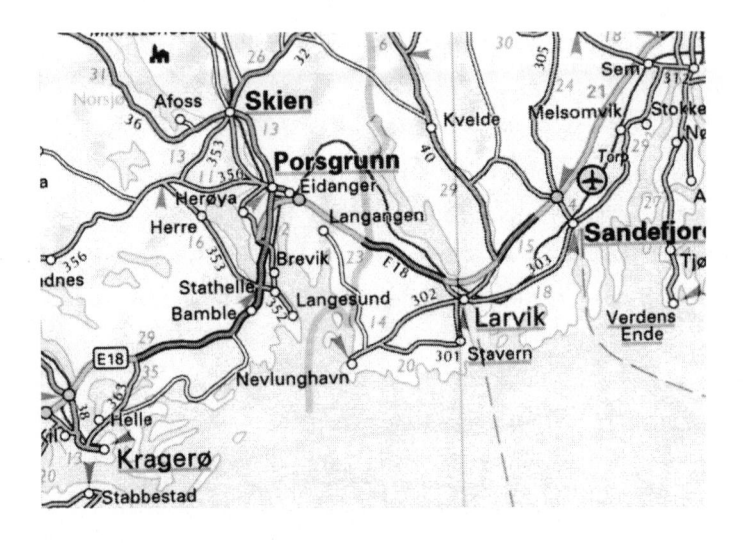

Post war he returned to work in Local Government but unable to stand its constraining atmosphere opted for a career in sales within the steel industry, specialising in agricultural and industrial wire products. Today, he lives where he started life almost ninety years ago, in Taunton and retains links with his flying days through membership of the Taunton & Tiverton Aircrew Association

He pulled 3 G's
GLIDERS, GAS & GUARDIAN of the SKIES!

Raymond Allan DREAN

An Ulsterman by birth, Ray was born near Londonderry in June 1924 but moved when orphaned to the mainland at the age of thirteen. On completion of his education he joined the RAF, initially through the Cardiff University Air Squadron. Flying from the Pengham Moor Airfield, to the East of the city, a variety of training aircraft were used of which one, Ray recalls, was the Miles Magister, featured below.

Initially Ray was very reluctant to talk about his service career as, like so many others, he felt that really there was not very much to say. Fortunately, in the end he agreed to speak and we learned that, leaving Cardiff in 1942, he joined the RAF 'proper' and after ITW in Paignton continued pilot training in South Africa. Successfully completing this, he was awarded his wings and awaited the long voyage back to the UK. By the time he arrived home it was 1944 and the war was entering a different phase, the main battlefront now being on mainland Europe. Keen to see action Ray volunteered, rather foolishly he now says, for the Glider Pilot Regiment.

His conversion from powered flight was undertaken at RAF Fairford where three types of glider were in operational use. These were the Hotspur, WACO Hadrian and the Horsa, the latter being a much larger development of the Hadrian. Pilots used to powered flight would look at their glider pilot colleagues in awe and wonder how anyone in the right mind would volunteer for such a job. In fact Ray almost proved them right for one night, taking off from Fairford, the tow rope linking him to the towing Albemarle broke. He could see the lights at Down Ampney in the distance and used these as a guide to keep his aircraft level. However, without the luxury of an engine, there was little he could do about his landing. In fact it ended in a ditch but not before he had hit and demolished a number of telephone wires!

Above: The Airspeed Horsa, a British Troop and cargo combat glider

Next posting was to join 'H' Squadron Glider Pilot Regiment with Nos. 296 and 297 Squadrons which had earlier played an active role in the invasion of Sicily. However, now the focus was on landings in Northern Europe and Ray found himself spending hours practising mass take-offs and landings. The rumour at the time was that they were being prepared for a mass airborne landing to capture the Kiel Canal in northern Germany but, despite all their training, this assault was never made.

Following the decision to abandon the Kiel landings, if indeed that had been the intended target, the need for airborne assaults in Germany largely disappeared and so, too, did Ray's role with the Glider Pilot Regiment.

Various other duties followed but, remaining in the RAF post war, one of the more interesting episodes of his service career was yet to come. With the end of hostilities, new roles were sought to harness the expertise of the many redundant aircrew. In fact the role chosen for Ray proved to be of such sensitivity that very few outside of those directly responsible knew of it.

It started when Ray found himself selected to undertake a number of lengthy courses, on completion of which he emerged with a new job title ... Explosives Officer! It was now 1946-47 and joining No.275 Maintenance Unit, he subsequently found himself deployed to No.2 Military Port at Cairnryan, a port on Scotland's western coast and situated on the shores of Loch Ryan which opens to the sea. It is a location now better known for its commercial ferry link between Scotland and Northern Ireland.

On arrival Ray became the Officer in Charge of large landing craft, one at a time, now no longer used to carry assault troops but for transporting explosives. This ordnance mainly comprised bombs of various sizes which were no longer required for the RAF & USAF bombing campaigns. Over sixty years ago Cairnryan was in a quiet and rather isolated location and thus ideal for the vessels selected to carry deadly cargoes to what was then believed to be an appropriate final resting place ... the deep trenches of the Irish Sea!

After many months in Scotland Ray moved south to Cumbria as the Commanding Officer of a detachment which took over the small port Silloth overlooking the Solway Firth.

Above: Ray checking bombs at Cairnryan before disposal in the Irish Sea

Looking back today at events of over sixty years ago one could arguably say this was to be the most controversial posting of Ray's RAF career for his new unit was destined to become the first selected for the disposal of Phosgene Gas bombs. Examination of a modern dictionary, or encyclopaedia, will help today's reader to understand the historic context of this. For instance, the Collins English Dictionary reads:

"Phosgene a colourless easily liquefied poisonous gas, carbonyl chloride, with an odour resembling new-mown hay: used in chemical warfare as a lethal choking agent ...... "

It is well known that the Nazis had the means to wage chemical warfare during WWII but, unlike during the First World War none of the warring powers did. Perhaps fear of reprisals was one of the factors behind this.

118

However the interesting fact to now emerge is that Britain did have a means of retaliation but what still remains today is the question of whether or not we would have used it. However, what we now know is that Ray played no small part in overseeing the ultimate destruction of our stock of Phosgene Gas bombs. Today, Ray will only say:

"It was all so long ago and just another job which had to be done. I was responsible for the two coastal vessels we used for their disposal, the 'Sir Evelyn Wood 'and the 'Malpacquet '. Our orders were to dump them in the depths of the Irish Sea which was considered the safest place and that's where they went. Since then, as far as I know, they have had no effect on marine life or any other aspects of the ecology although I very much doubt if the same means of disposal would be used today."

Ray did eventually return to flying, spending five years as a student at University College and Chelsea College whilst flying such aircraft as the Harvard with the University of London Air Squadron. Positions with Hawker Aircraft and English Electric as Inspector and Stress Engineer followed after flying ceased but perhaps his biggest career change came in 1957 when he answered an advert for 'pilots and navigators' and was to spend the last twenty-seven years of his working life with the Civil Aviation Authority as an Air Traffic Controller. Initially this was at Croydon Airfield controlling, as Ray once described, 'real aircraft', before Gatwick opened. After Croydon, several other airports and the Scottish Control Centre - Oceanic Control (radar), before ending his career at Manston, part of the London Air Traffic Control Centre.

When retirement came Ray and his wife, Pat, moved to Torbay but did not completely sever links with his past life for he is a member of the Aircrew Association and supports the East Devon members in many of their events.

The SHRAPNEL KID ... at 91

Edward H, FROST

Ted Frost was born in the London Borough of Ealing in March 1920 and educated locally. During his latter educational years, which included night school, he concentrated on commercial subjects such as accountancy, with the ultimate aim of becoming a Chartered Accountant. In fact his first job on leaving school was in the Accounts Department of the U.S. owned Quaker Oats Company. Despite starting an accountancy based career Ted also had a long standing interest in flying which had been kindled at the age of six when given a flight in the rear cockpit of a WWI Avro 504K bi-plane. It was therefore no surprise to his family when, in 1937, he enrolled in the RAFVR and commenced training as a pilot on Tiger Moths. This took most of his spare time at weekends and also summer camps at Halton and Kidlington in Oxfordshire.

The declaration of war in September 1939 quickly saw the complete mobilisation of the RAFVR and by the end of the year Ted was serving full time within the Royal Air Force. With his pilot training completed he was initially posted to RAF Hendon to fly the Lysander in an army co-operation role which involved flying set courses at varying altitudes to assist the training of gun crews which ultimately would be used for the defence of Britain against air attacks. However this role drastically changed during, and after, the retreat from Dunkirk. Then their role was two-fold. Firstly they searched for downed aircrew in the Channel but, more importantly, their Lysander aircraft were ideally suited for clandestine missions into occupied France. These involved the dropping and recovery of secret agents, known only to Ted as 'Joes', often from fields where their landing path was illuminated by members of the resistance holding torches. But as Ted now says: *"After a few months the appeal of this type of operation lost its attraction so when Bomber Command asked for aircrew to fill the substantial losses they were sustaining I decided to put my name forward. As a Londoner, and seeing what the Germans were doing to my city, and others, the idea of giving them some of their own back appealed to me."*

Ted's application to transfer was accepted. However, first he had to learn how to fly twin-engine aircraft so after a quick course on the Anson he arrived at OTU, Kinloss, Scotland, for further training on the Whitley. It was an aircraft he said he 'grew to like' and it was also here they formed their crews before moving south to Lincolnshire and the Heavy Conversion Unit (HCU) at RAF Swinderby. Here they were introduced to the Avro Manchester. Whilst ideal for the purpose of converting aircrew to fly heavy bombers, the Manchester itself has been labelled as *'one of the greatest disappointments of the Second World War'*. Although designed as a heavy bomber, it was still a twin-engine aircraft and these proved to be not only underpowered but were also unreliable, traits which made it completely unsuitable for its intended role. Only 159 Manchesters were built but, on a more positive note, the airframe proved excellent and it was this aspect of the aircraft which was carried forward to its successor, the Avro Lancaster.

With HCU completed, Ted was posted to No.61 Squadron which was based at Syerston and operated the Lancaster Mk.3 heavy bomber. He recalls their sister Squadron, No.106, was still flying the Hampden and their C.O. was Wg.Cdr. Guy Gibson who later, flying the Lancaster as C.O. of No.617 Squadron, was to be awarded the VC following their famous Dambuster raid.

Above: The greatly under-powered twin-engine Manchester

Ted vividly recalls his first operational flight was to bomb the Focke-Wulf aircraft works at Neuenland and described how their wireless operator collected two carrier pigeons from their loft before making for the aircraft. There was a last cigarette for the smokers and, he says, the last minute 'pee' on the tail wheel 'for luck'!   On crossing the coast the gunners checked their guns and, now on oxygen, they were flying at 19000 feet and still climbing to their operational height.   On this particular raid they were accompanied by a Canadian pilot who gave rise to a minor language misunderstanding which Ted remembers to this day.   This arose on approaching the German border when the rear gunner reported over the intercom there was defensive activity ahead which led to the Canadian's responsive drawl of   "Jeesse, I didn't expect to see blackbirds at this altitude." In fact what the rear gunner had reported was 'flak bursts'!

Ted was to make many more excursions into Germany. During a raid on Saarbruken the flak was particularly heavy and they returned with a 'few holes' in their aircraft. Next came a raid on Dusseldorf, the city being very heavily defended with even heavier flak and also against them was the fact it was a clear moonlit night which helped the enemy night fighters. They lost four of their aircraft on this raid.   Other heavily defended targets followed and these included Karlsruhe, Nuremburg and Munich.

A change of tactics came in August 1942 when intelligence reports suggested that the German heavy cruiser, the Prinz Eugen', would try to leave her Baltic port and make for the Atlantic. Ted's squadron was one of those tasked with laying mines in the Baltic to thwart her passage and recalls: *"it was a new experience for us, flying very low over the sea at a speed just above stalling. There was also intensive anti-aircraft fire from flak ships but the real shock came later. That was when we discovered that such trips only counted as ½ an 'op' towards the thirty needed for a rest!"*

Now part of the unique Pathfinder Force, in October 1942, the Squadron practiced extensive low level formation flying and bomb dropping. Later, as a group of twelve squadrons, they learned their target was to be the Schneider - le Creusot works, one of Europe's largest steel works which was producing heavy calibre guns, locomotives and heavy castings. Code named 'Operation Robinson' the reason for their low flying practice became evident. Flying as three Wings, the twelve squadrons flew over Lands End at 1000 feet then gradually lost height to cross the French coast near the Ile d'Yeu at only 100 feet. This tree-top height was maintained for the next 300 miles across France until reaching their target about 90 miles from Geneva. With 40 miles to go, they gradually gained height to their bombing altitude of around 5000 feet, taking the enemy completely by surprise. It was now dusk and the entire raid was over in about ten minutes. Ted also made two raids on Berlin in January of 1943, the first made difficult due to snow but the second, in bright moonlight, resulted in the loss of 22 aircraft. However, not all raids resulted in a return to base in the UK as he explains. Describing one such raid on the Zeppelin sheds at Friedrickshaven, which was a main producer of radar components, he said that from there they continued to North Africa, landing at a US base near Algiers. Then, on the return leg home, they bombed Milan in Northern Italy.

Arguably, his most memorable 'op' was the bombing of the Skoda works at Pilsen when he describes the flak as extremely heavy with large numbers of enemy night fighters also evident. Problems started when flak hit their aircraft on the way to the target, damaging their starboard inner engine which began to overheat and lose power. The only solution was to feather it and continue on. Then, making their bombing run, the aircraft suffered more hits before dropping its bomb load on target and quickly setting course for home. But that was not quite the end of their ordeal for they were then attacked by a Ju88 night fighter. Cannon shells ripped through the fuselage, killing their rear gunner, fatally wounding the mid-upper gunner and also severely wounding Ted. Despite considerable damage, and his injuries, Ted managed to get the crippled aircraft home on three engines only for the starboard undercarriage to collapse immediately on landing. As soon as the aircraft spun to a halt Ted and his crew made a rapid evacuation. He had completed his tour of 'ops' and, already 'mentioned in despatches', for his leadership and courage he was now deservedly awarded the DFC. However, as we shall read later, he was also to be affected by his wounds for many years to come, although after a period of rest he was to return to flying.

Having once described all his operations as falling into one of four categories, viz. 'Dodgy', 'Frightening', 'Scary' or 'Terrifying', his experience was put to good use as an instructor at No.29 Operational Conversion Unit (OCU) at RAF Bruntingford. Here, under his watchful eye, new crews were put through their paces on the Wellington.

When hostilities ended a further task awaited the RAF, that of bringing home troops from the various war zones and also to repatriate liberated POWs. Ted was posted to Transport Command to fly Liberators based at RAF Oakington and spent the next few months flying to and from India bringing troops home from the Far East.

Completing his service as a Flight Lieutenant, Ted returned to his pre-war post with the Quaker Oat Company. However, the prospect of an office bound career no longer appealed but, fortunately, he was offered a new role within the sales department. Quickly accepting the new challenge, he was to rise to become Sales Development Director, a senior position involving visits to their international HQ in Chicago.

Sadly now a widower after 64 years of marriage, retirement brought him and his family to the peaceful hamlet of Nicholashayne, on the border of Devon and Somerset. He has not lost his love of numbers and still occasionally helps with his son's accountancy business and also reminisces about his RAF days with fellow members of the Taunton and Tiverton Aircrew Association.

However, we cannot let his story end without one last twist. In May 2011, at the age of 91, he was interviewed for this book shortly after returning home from his umpteenth visit to hospital. Always the reasons for these visits are the same .... the removal of more fragments of shrapnel from his chest, a lasting souvenir of his wartime encounter with a Luftwaffe Ju88 night fighter over Nazi Germany.

Above: The versatile JU 88. A night fighter fitted with the 'Schrage Musik' cannon and the cause of Ted's injuries

TRAINED by the UNITED STATES NAVY

Laurence GREATHEAD

Laurie, a native of County Durham, was born in early March 1923 and after completing his education locally became a clerk within the chemical industry. At the age of nineteen he volunteered for aircrew duties and, as a result, on the 9th November 1942, reported to an Aircrew Reception Centre in London.

Assessed suitable for further training as a pilot, Laurie undertook basic training at an Initial Training Wing (ITW) at Cambridge where accommodation was in the university's colleges and his particular billet was in Magdalene. Relating to this particular aspect of training he prefers to forget the more serious side in favour of the sporting pursuits where he opted for a Cambridge favourite ... rowing! As a member of an 'eight' he says it was very enjoyable although he had a few reservations when they became involved with the 'Lent Bumper Races'. He explained these as:

"Basically the procedure was that all of the colleges had a place on the river and when the signal was given the objective was to bump the boat in front of yours and if you succeeded you changed places. Over a period of time the fastest would become Head of the River, "

Completing ITW, his next posting was to No.18 EFTS (Elementary Flying

Training School) at Fairoaks, Surrey, for 10 hours flying on Tiger Moths. Completing his first 'solo' within this time confirmed his suitability for continued training as a pilot so, after three weeks at an Aircrew Dispersal Centre in Manchester, he set sail across the Atlantic to Canada where the next three weeks were spent at Moncton, New Brunswick, waiting for the venue for the next stage of training which was to be in the United States.

On the 15th May 1944, he arrived at the US Naval Air Training Centre at Grosse Isle, near Detroit, where he undertook primary training on the Stearman, a single engine biplane.

Left: The US Navy's primary trainer, the Stearman. It had a top speed of 124 mph. service ceiling was quoted as 11,200 feet and range 505 miles.

It was a very versatile aircraft and is still used for stunt flying today. In fact Laurie recalls that they were put through quite an intense course of aerobatics which suggested that their course was identical to that for carrier based fighter aircraft. However it is the American drawl which still sticks in his mind with the "Yer gar it "or "I gar it" when control of the aircraft passed between him and the instructor! Following completion of primary flying at Grosse Isle, Laurie found himself travelling to the other end of the United States to the US Naval Base at Pensacola in Florida for advanced flying training. This was undertaken on Catalina PBY-5 flying boats. On the 11th May 1944, with total of 215 hours in his log book, he was awarded pilot's wings, both RAF and US Navy, and headed north again, to Canada and the voyage back to the UK.

Left: The Catalina, a versatile aircraft used by both the USN and RAF for anti-submarine patrols in the Pacific, Indian and Atlantic Oceans

Although return to the UK was straightforward, Laurie then faced the same situation as many aircrew qualifying at this period of the war, the lack of vacancies for operational flying. The high losses experienced previously, which had lead to the rapid expansion of aircrew training, had lessened considerably as the war tipped decidedly in the Allies favour. Initially, just to keep his recently acquired skills in practice, Laurie found himself sent to No.11 EFTS, near Perth, to once again fly the Tiger Moth. However, his stay was short, only ten days, and then he was posted to No.21 Advanced Flying Unit (AFU) at Tatenhill for a return to twin-engine flying on the Airspeed Oxford.

Right: The Airspeed Oxford. The aircraft shown here, R6026, was flown by CACCU at Exeter in 1955

Leaving Tatenhill on the 2nd October 1944, three more short postings came in quick succession before arriving at No.2 FIS, Montrose, on the 27th December 1944 to undertake an instructor's course. Successfully completing this, his next move was to join No.20 (P) AFU at Weston-on-the-Green as an instructor. It was whilst there that the end of the war in Europe came and with it the end of Laurie's flying. He had 529 hours in his log book.

However, it was not the end of his RAF service and there was still a problem of what to do with redundant pilots. Laurie now explains one solution:

"*Someone must have said 'desert', for having been sent by train through France and shipped across the Med to Egypt, that is exactly where we found ourselves ... for six weeks under canvas, at Kasfareet. Then I was on the move again, firstly to Almaza, and then on the 13th December 1945 I found myself at RAF Lydda in Palestine where I had the job title of 'Load Controller'. The station was a staging post for RAF Transport Command and, although relatively quiet, we did carry revolvers for a while and two aircraft belonging to the Comms Flight were destroyed. Nevertheless we did manage the odd escape and on one occasion two of us hitched a lift to the Lebanon and were able to visit Beirut although I was not greatly impressed. At one point a cry went out that they wanted all pilots back flying but my thoughts were unprintable. By now I just wanted to get out, a wish that came true on the 29th October 1946 when I began the long journey home, arriving at RAF Warton on the 7th December. I was demobbed on the 20th December 1946, and was home just in time for Christmas.*"

Like many young men starting their aircrew training around 1942-43, Laurie's dreams of operational flying were never fully realised. Delays in training, followed by diminished operational requirements, thwarted their early aspirations. Nevertheless, their role was invaluable for they were trained and there if ever needed. Leaving the RAF Laurie returned to his former employers and was later to qualify as a Management Accountant (ACMA), remaining with them until he retired in 1982. Today he lives with his wife, Patricia, in Plymouth and is a member of the local aircrew luncheon club as well as the East Devon Aircrew Association.

UNDER AGE PILOT!

Terence W GREEN

Born at Woking, Surrey, in March 1924, Terry was educated at Holy Trinity Boys' School, Chelsea, not far from the family's mews flat which came with his father's employment. Leaving school at fourteen, he remained at home with his parents having found employment as a warehouseman. Soon to experience the London Blitz, fate conspired against them on a number of fronts, one being loss of jobs. The family decided to move back to Surrey and a new home relatively close to Brooklands Race Track, the site of two aircraft factories. These were for Hawker and Vickers Armstrong and it was not long before young Terry found employment helping with the assembly of Wellington bombers. A military target, on the 6th September 1940 German Me. Bf 110s paid a daylight visit whilst he was working there, killing eighty-three of his work colleagues and leaving an indelible imprint of carnage on his young mind.

His mind quickly turned from building aircraft to flying them, except there were two great hurdles. Firstly he was only 16½ years of age and, having left school at fourteen, had no educational qualifications. Nevertheless, exaggerating his age, he duly presented himself as potential aircrew. To his surprise he passed the examinations and medical and was assessed suitable for pilot training. However he soon discovered that the RAF did not always respond with alacrity and for the next couple of months found himself shuffled between stations doing odd jobs. Finally, in May 1941, he arrived at an ITW at Babbacombe, Torquay, for initial studies before moving to nearby Paignton for the second stage of the course. To his surprise on its completion he was the only one to be selected for pilot training in the USA.

Crossing the Atlantic to Canada on the M.S. Stratheden was followed by an overland route, via Toronto, to Albany in the Southern US State of Georgia. They were now in 'civvies', recognising the fact that the USA was still a neutral country. Initial flying was at the civilian Darr Aero Technical College, under contract to the US Government, and the aircraft flown was the Stearman, a bi-plane not unlike the RAF's Tiger Moth. Then moving to a USAAF base at Macon, flying continued on the Vultee 13A until finally progressing to the more powerful and technically advanced North American AT-6.

Left: The Vultee 13A. Similar in looks to the AT-6 but with a less powerful engine and fixed undercarriage

It was whilst flying an AT-6, known as the Texan in the US and the Harvard in the UK, that Terry experienced his first accident. This occurred when his engine failed shortly after take-off and, at only 300 feet, he had little alternative but to land wheels-up straight ahead. Fortunately he survived unscathed. Then, half way through the course, there was a momentous change when, on the 7th December 1941, the Japanese navy attacked the US fleet at Pearl Harbour, bringing the US into the war. Immediately 'civvies' were replaced by RAF uniform. Finally it was Graduation Day and Terry was awarded his pilot's wings three weeks before his eighteenth birthday!

Returning to the UK, he attended No.57 Spitfire OCU at Hawarden before being posted to 10 Group, No.501 Squadron, based at Middle Wallop and equipped with the Spitfire Mk5. However his stay in Hampshire was short for soon after his arrival the Squadron deployed to Northern Ireland for a six month break from 'ops' with their flying mainly anti-submarine surveillance patrols between the ports of Belfast and Liverpool. Terry, as a newcomer, did not need a rest and this was rectified by a posting to Algiers in North Africa where, shortly after arrival, he found himself at the controls of a Hurricane for the first time. Unfortunately, for the second time he suffered engine failure, this time whilst coming into land. The Hurricane did not make the runway and Terry described the result as *"the Hurricane was in a bit of a mess!"*. He walked away from the wreckage to learn he was to join No.232 Squadron to fly the familiar Spitfire Mk.5, Initially from Tingley but later from a landing strip very close to the front line at Souk-el-Khemis.

Here all resemblance to flying from bases in the UK ceased. No more comfortable messes, decent food and trips to the pub or cinema. Now it was four to a tent with all pilots sharing the same primitive dining conditions. However morale remained high. Terry soon settled in with his new Squadron, little knowing at the time he would progress from their rookie pilot to one of their longest serving. Baptism came quick, for operating only a few seconds flying time from the British 1st Army's front line, he soon encountered a couple of Fw. 190's. They were faster than his Spitfire but he could out turn them and their meeting ended 'honours even'! Sorties came fast and furious, many playing escort to the Boston, a medium bomber, and Hurricanes being used in a fighter/bomber role. Others involved strafing enemy troop concentrations and transport. Such forays did not come without casualties with the squadron losing twelve pilots in one three week spell, three being killed during a night raid on the base by JU88s. Enemy flak was a constant problem and Terry relates how, flying with a new Flight

Commander, they were soon in deep trouble. Escorting a squadron of Bostons, they encountered intense ground fire resulting in the Flight Commander and another pilot being killed and a third being shot down but surviving. Of the four escorting aircraft Terry was the only one to return. The following day he was airborne again, this time to see the 'Hurribomber' he was escorting blow up in front of him.

In May 1943 Tunis fell and with the war in North Africa virtually over No.232 Squadron were stood down for a seven-day rest. Then it was Malta and once again sleeping within four walls. Re-united with his trusty Spitfire he found the enemy's new tactics rather confusing. It seemed they wanted to avoid any contact for, although their Me 109s and Fw 190s were faster, on seeing any Spitfires they made a hasty retreat and never engaged in combat. However, by August 1943, a new front was opening with the Allied invasion of Sicily and soon afterwards No.232 Squadron was operating from the island. But this was just a springboard for a landing on Italy itself when Terry and his colleagues gave cover to the Royal Navy, who were bombarding enemy shore positions, as well as carrying out a few strafing sorties of their own.

Above: Two of his adversaries   Left: the Me Bf 109 and, right, the Fw 190

The main assault was still to come, the Allied landing at Salerno. From their base in Sicily this raised a logistical problem ... enough fuel for a 175 mile flight to the target area then the same distance home again. This was solved by adding 90 gallon overload tanks to the aircraft, thus providing over three hours flying time. One problem still remained. With the tanks the Spitfire was less manoeuvrable so if an enemy was spotted on route to the target did the pilot jettison to give himself a better chance in combat and, if doing so, would there be enough fuel to get home? However once the beachhead had been established the problem was solved although another one arose. The Squadron now moved to a small rudimentary airstrip which was actually situated in front of our own artillery and only a few hundred yards from the enemy's. Shells from both sides often rained overhead although, fortunately, no Spitfire was ever hit. Not that they did not suffer damage. The strip was too short for normal landings and soon became even shorter when piles of broken Spitfires grew at both ends. Luckily they soon moved again!

As they advanced across Italy the Squadron's role remained the same, jointly carrying out raids of their own or escorting US Mitchell bombers on theirs. It was now early 1944 and 322 Fighter Wing, of which 232 was part, was split up with two of the squadrons moving to India. For 232 it was Syria. Terry later learned that their move was part of a plan to encourage Turkey to enter the war against the Nazis but when they did not after six weeks the Squadron moved again. It was now Palestine and re-equipping with the Spitfire Mk9. Again the stay was short ... next move, Corsica. They continued their raids on Italy and one, an attack on the railway yard at Livorno, was almost Terry's last. Encountering heavy flak, he was not aware of any damage to his Spitfire but its engine began to play-up. It was touch and go whether he would make it back to base and he almost didn't, crashing a few yards short of the runway. His log book records: *"Both wings ripped off, one in two pieces, tail plane just hanging on."* Fortunately he was only shaken not hurt.

Shortly after, on the 13th August 1944, there was another milestone when he was chosen to lead the whole Squadron for a raid on a German radar station near Marseilles. Again he had a narrow escape, this time flak putting two holes in his wing and another shell piercing the engine cowling. Fortunately it missed the essential parts and he returned safely to base. Following the successful Allied landing in the South of France, Terry moved to the mainland, firstly to a base near Frejus and later North up the Rhone Valley. It was September 1944 and he was now, bar one, the Squadron's longest serving pilot and had moved with them twenty-three times since first joining them in North Africa. Sad news followed, the Squadron was to be disbanded but there was also good news. He had been commissioned, his promotion back dated to 6th August 1944. Many posts were to follow, the first taking him back to Naples where he contracted malaria, and then to Cairo but none could compare with his days with No.232 Squadron. Demobilised in 1946 he became a Management Trainee with the Amalgamated Dental Company at Walton-on-Thames and still managed to fly as a member of the RAFVR. In 1966, his work brought him to the West Country where with Edna, his wife, he set up home in Bridgwater and later became an active member of the Taunton & Tiverton Aircrew Association.

He has put his RAF exploits into book form which one day he hopes to see published. There is no way his many experiences could be covered in these few pages. However, to summarise, one could say:

For a lad who left school at fourteen with no qualifications, became a pilot before he was eighteen, served in four Continents, visited thirteen countries, flew over 150 operational sorties over enemy territory in a Spitfire and added another hundred hours in a Hurricane, one can only say ...

Didn't he do well!

JOIN the ARMY .... SEE the WORLD!

Andrew R. HATFIELD

Although born in Nottingham in June 1976, Andrew is very much a Devonian at heart, moving to Exmouth in 1985 at the age of nine and subsequently becoming a pupil at Exmouth Community College. On completing his education his mind was already set on an Army career, no doubt influenced to some extent by his elder brother who was serving with the Army Air Corps. It was no surprise, therefore, when in April 1995 he joined the Army Training Regiment at Winchester to commence his service with the Army Air Corps.

After further training at Middle Wallop, in November 1995 he was posted to 661Squadron, 1 Regiment, Army Air Corps based at Gutersloh in Germany. Initially, as ground crew, his role was to support the squadron's Lynx and Gazelle helicopters. Although the posting was for a three year period, any illusions that this would be spent entirely in Germany were quickly dispelled. However, unfortunately for the reader, having only recently left the Armed Forces, and having served in areas where there was recent or still on-going conflict, Andrew has been subject to many restrictions under the Official Secrets Act so some of the finer details must be left to the imagination.

However, we know that from his base in Germany he was to spend time in Canada, Kenya, Cyprus, Poland and the Balkans. Invariably these moves involved a variety of training exercises but also included a six month detachment to No.5 Regiment Army Air Corps in Northern Ireland which operated Islander aircraft in a surveillance role. He also completed a parachute course at Bangor.

Left: A surveillance version of the Army Air Corps Islander

As if it had not been exciting before, in November 1998 it became more so when he was posted to 8 Flight at Sterling Lines, Hereford, a town synonymous with the SAS. He was now classified as 'loadmaster', an aircrew category which made him responsible for all internal operations within the aircraft other than actually flying it. It was a small unit comprising four Augusta 109 helicopters and two Gazelles. Interestingly, two of the Augustas had been captured from the Argentine Forces during the Falklands War. At this time, as support to the SAS, he remained on standby to attend any anti-terrorist operation in the UK or abroad. Needless to say, many hours were also spent on training exercises. However Andrew was involved in one anti-terrorist incident for real. This occurred in February 2000 when an airliner hi-jacked by Afghans landed at Stansted Airport. Andrew was one of the first on the scene.

The stand-off lasted five days which he says *'although tense was very exciting'*. Another period of excitement came in the June whilst undertaking exercises in France with their Special Forces. Using explosives, one device broke loose and hit the tail of their aircraft, an incident of which he now says: *"By God did I close my eyes ... one of my nine lives lost!"*

Above (left) is an Army Air Corps Augusta A109, this particular aircraft now being retired to the Army Air Corps Museum at Middle Wallop. Right: An AAC Lynx Mk 7 on the ice in Arctic Norway.

By now Andrew was nearing the end of his two year tour with the SAS, which he says had been a very exciting challenge, and was looking for a similar role. His prayers were answered when he heard the Army was forming a new squadron at RAF Odiham to operate as a 'Joint Special Forces Aviation Wing' and was to be equipped with seven RAF Chinook helicopters and six AAC Lynx helicopters. He applied to join the unit and in January 2001 his wish came true when he joined 657 Squadron which was unique for it operated away from the mainstream AAC. Again he found himself operating in support of the SAS and now, additionally, the SBS.

There was also constant training in readiness for any emergency which may arise. On the itinerary was Norway, for arctic training and also, by contrast, shortly after a deployment to the Oman where the temperature was above 50 degrees C. The mere touching of the aircraft's metal could burn your hands. However, there were other dangers and during live-firing exercises two of the troops were accidentally killed and a third badly injured. In September 2002 Andrew briefly returned to Northern Ireland to complete an air-gunners course and later, on returning to 657 Squadron, to convert onto the 50 calibre machine gun which was unique to their squadron's Lynx aircraft. Able to fire 6 rounds per second from its 1200 round magazine, it was deadly accurate up to 1km.

In November 2002 training increased and rumours circulated about a possible invasion of Iraq. Two months later they were in Cyprus where the squadron was divided into two, one half staying in Cyprus and the other, which included Andrew, moving to Jordan to join up with the SAS. Then came the invasion itself during which they undertook many operations with the Special Forces, particularly in the Basra area, including a visit to Saddam's palace.

However, by the June their helicopters had flown many hours in adverse conditions and needed urgent repairs and replacement engines. Returning to the UK there was also some welcome leave. Then, in October 2003, it was off to South America for jungle training in Guyana. They returned home in the December, once again to experience extremes of temperature with a return visit to Norway for more arctic training. Andrew explained that 657 was the only AAC squadron which specialised in arctic warfare so it was necessary to retain their skills. However after four weeks they were brought home again. There was another assignment awaiting them.

It was now March 2004 and two of the squadron's Lynx aircraft were prepared for their next move ... to Afghanistan! Here Andrew and his colleagues initially operated out of Kabul where, co-operating with Special Forces, their role was to locate and destroy the opium fields which were helping to fund the Taliban, Afghanistan being the world's largest producer.

He says he found the tour extremely interesting, not only for the work but also for the dramatic scenery and the culture. He also says that during their patrols they often spotted old equipment abandoned by the Russians during their ill-fated stay in the country.

Above: Andrew checking the M3M Browning 50 calibre machine gun on his Lynx Mk7 and below: patrolling over Afghanistan during 2004.

With his six month tour completed Andrew returned to the UK for some well earned rest but two months later, in January 2005, he was once again to return to a 'war zone'. This time it was back to Iraq, their aircraft now fitted with the latest surveillance equipment which had been purchased from Canada. Their role was mainly patrolling over Baghdad and Fallujah, often flying as low as 30 feet to seek out and capture insurgents.

The dangers faced by our Forces in such environments cannot be overstated and Andrew relates two such incidents during this period. He says, *"We lost our Hercules C130 during this tour when it was shot down north of Baghdad and I was probably the last British serviceman to see the crew alive. I had been at the airport on 'standby' when I saw it discharge some troops before taking off again. About twenty minutes later we heard the call, 'Albert is down', Albert being the aircraft's call sign. We immediately scrambled our two Lynx with Special Forces and were the first to arrive on the scene. I remember seeing the Hercules smashed apart and on fire. No one had survived. All ten crew had been killed."*

The second incident he mentions was, ironically, his last operation before returning to the UK and he was flying with his relief crew. It was 4 a.m. and they were returning to base when they came under small arms fire whilst over the capital. He explained to his replacement it was something he would get used to! In March 2005 he returned to RAF Odiham, having decided to leave the Service at the ten year mark. After some resettlement training and leave Andrew was finally demobilised in the July.

Today, happily married to Sarah, whom he has known since he was twelve years old, and with a young family, he is the Business Manager for a main dealership in the motor industry. However, he still remains in touch with many of his former service friends and often goes to re-unions of 657 Squadron and 8 Flight at Hereford. He is also a keen member of the East Devon Aircrew Association. Of his action packed years in the Army he says,

"I had a great time and would recommend it to anyone".

NAVIGATOR? First Try PIGS, POTATOES & POST!!!

Desmond HINCHLIFF

This is the intriguing tale of a young lad who, in January 1943, was accepted for aircrew training but then spent the next two years doing anything but!

Des Hinchliff was born in Holmfirth, West Yorkshire, in March 1925 and, following a Grammar School education, joined ICI as a laboratory assistant. In early summer 1942, at 17 ¼ years of age, the earliest age permissible, he volunteered for aircrew duties. However, it was the end of the year before he was called for a medical examination with interviews following on the 6th January 1943 when he was assessed suitable for training as pilot, navigator or bomb aimer and enlisted into the RAFVR.

Des's story is an interesting one, not because of daring exploits and aerial battles but because it illustrates how disorganised the RAF could appear at times. It was six months later, on the 12th July, before he was actually mobilised and told to report for a further medical and issue of uniform at St. John's Wood Aircrew Reception Centre in London. Meals were taken in the restaurant of London Zoo and memories of the animals subsequently made him think of how pigs delayed the start of his aircrew training as he now explains:

"I was, with others, detailed to take part in various extraneous activities which included being transported on a daily basis to what was referred to as the RAF pig farm at Slip End near Markyate in Hertfordshire. Here we spent the day mucking out and feeding the animals. Another chore we had was

'household and gardening activities' at Winfield House in Regents Park which was the official residence of the American Ambassador. However, what was particularly galling was the fact that at the same time Germany was attacking London with their V-1 flying bombs. I suppose you could say the only excitement we had was taking evasive action when they fell close to where we undertook PE in Regents Park!"

It was now February 1944 and a year had passed since Des had been accepted for aircrew training. However things were beginning to stir and the first stage of his training started in earnest when he was posted to No.6 Initial Training Wing (ITW), at the Marine Hotel, Aberystwyth. Here there was more PE with hours of drill on the Esplanade but, more importantly, there was intensive study of subjects such as elementary navigation, meteorology, principles of flight etc. When the course was completed the next move was to No.3 Elementary Flying Training School (EFTS) at Shellingford, Oxfordshire.

This was for 'grading', a stage in selection which defined one's future aircrew category and was basically twelve hours flying in a Tiger Moth during which time practical skills were assessed. For instance many would-be pilots, although passing tests on the ground, found they lacked the ability to judge distances between the air and ground, so necessary when trying to land an aircraft.

For those lacking the necessary 'spatial awareness' training would continue as navigators or bomb aimers, both equally important roles in a bomber crew as the latter would take over as navigator in the event of serious injury or death.

Above: The de Havilland Tiger Moth
It was used for aircrew 'grading' and also as an elementary trainer.

Des left Shellingford on the 6th June 1944, a date indelibly etched in his mind for it was D-day, and returned to ACRC, London, to be told he would be trained as a navigator. However a further six months passed before training started and how he spent this period is, again, beyond comprehension. Briefly he spent some time at RAF Padgate, Lancashire, where his task was 'potato picking'! Then there was assisting the Post Office to sort the 1944 Christmas mail when it arrived at one of Manchester's railway stations!

In fairness, however, one temporary posting to RAF Waterbeach in Cambridgeshire did provide some excitement. It was home to No.514 Squadron which flew the Lancaster and Des had been attached to the radar section to become marginally involved in servicing some of the squadron's navigational aids. He describes one event as follows:

"I was alone in the section when a telephone call from one of the flight offices requested immediate assistance because one of the Lancasters at dispersal was billowing smoke which appeared to be issuing from the 'Gee'

box (a navigational aid). So I jumped into a spare vehicle, although I had no driving experience, and managed to cross the airfield and home-in on the offending aircraft. The fuselage was full of smoke but no obvious fire detected! So what to do? Well, I climbed into the aircraft, isolated the smoking box, and rapidly deposited it on the grass. The aircraft was declared safe and I felt pretty good!"

It was now early January 1945 and at last Des could look forward to his navigator training with some degree of expectation. He was posted to Canada and set sail on the Dutch ship, the 'Nieuw Amsterdam', which he said was quite fast and made the Atlantic crossing without being in a convoy or having an escort. However, his recollections of the voyage are worth recording and were described as follows:

"The crossing took about eight days and the weather was pretty awful. I think there were six of us to a cabin which did not help much as most of us were seasick at some time or another. Other passengers were German POW's, whom we were supposed to guard, many of whom were seasick as well, also American G.I's returning home who seemed to spend a lot of their time playing 'craps' on deck!"

The ship docked in New York from where the RAF trainees travelled North by train to RCAF Moncton in Nova Scotia where they were kitted out with winter clothing. From there Canadian National Railways took a northern route through the backwoods of Ontario and after a two day journey they arrived at their ultimate destination, the RCAF's No.7 Air Observer School at Portage la Prairie, Manitoba, although not long after his arrival it was renamed as No.3 Air Navigation School. Des says little about the mysteries of navigator training except that he enjoyed it and the flying element of their training was undertaken in the Mk.1 Anson which required around 130 turns on the handle to wind up the undercarriage!

Another important date was 7th May 1945 when V-E Day was declared and they were still to finish the course. Speculation was rife. Would they actually complete training and join a Squadron or maybe continue to become part of Tiger Force, the planned final assault on the Japanese.

On the other hand would the course be closed? In fact it continued to its completion at the end of June and Des was awarded his long awaited Navigator's brevet. On the 1st July 1945 they boarded a Canadian Pacific train which took them to join the Cunard liner, the Aquitania, for the voyage back to England. A period of leave followed and then it was 15th August 1945, VJ Day, also another date in Des's memory for it was the day he was posted to No.4 EFTS Brough, East Yorkshire.

Accompanied by other newly trained pilots and navigators he was to spend the next few weeks flying around in ancient Tiger Moths whilst decisions were made as to their future deployment. Two minor detachments to RAF Lyneham and the Aircrew Holding Unit at Cranage was followed by the news that further navigator training was suspended. With demobilisation not due until 1946 the RAF then took steps towards helping redundant aircrew towards post-war employment. With Des's pre-war laboratory training, after an introductory course he was posted to the Pathology Laboratory at RAF Hospital, St. Athan in South Wales. Here he met two other technicians both, like him, being ex-aircrew, one a pilot the other a navigator. The laboratory was under the charge of a single pathologist. His account s of analysing blood, sputum, faeces and urine are too graphic to fully recount here although one macabre incident which occurred whilst he was later on duty at RAF Hospital, Yatesbury, is perhaps worth a mention. Here he relates it in his own words:

"An admin officer had died unexpectedly and a post mortem had to be performed at the station. Thus for the first and last time I found myself

assisting the pathologist in carrying out the post mortem. The weather was freezing and we were wearing white smocks over our greatcoats. I recall using a half-pint glass tankard as one of my 'instruments' but prudence prohibits me from saying what it was used for. It was quite an experience!"

Des left the RAF on the 15th April 1947 and rejoined ICI. After pursuing further studies he qualified as a Chartered Chemical Engineer and became involved in the management of chemical plants. As his expertise grew so did his responsibilities. In 1966 he was appointed the Chief Alkali and Radiochemical Inspector for Northern Ireland, a statutory appointment, and a position he held for almost twenty years. He also became a Fellow of both the Chemical Engineering and Energy Institutes and a Member of the Society for Radiological Protection. He left Northern Ireland in 1985 when asked by the Government of Oman to help establish the first Ministry of the Environment in the Middle East. He was there during the time of the Russian Chernobyl nuclear incident which then involved him in advisory meetings in Saudi Arabia and Iraq. Returning to England in 1989, he became a Consultant in Environmental Control which entailed word-wide travel. The Royal Air Force may have missed his leadership potential but post war the scientific world certainly did not!

Eventually with Nancy, his wife for sixty years, Desmond settled in Devon's Dartmoor village of Yelverton where his garden was only yards from the perimeter of former RAF Harrowbeer. He rekindled his RAF connections by joining the Plymouth Branch of the Aircrew Association, later joining the East Devon membership when the former branch ceased.

Recently he and Nancy moved to Bath to be closer to their family but Des still retains his membership and keeps in touch with his East Devon colleagues.

DOWN IN THE DRINK ... OFF LUNDY

Ivan C.J. HUGHES

Born in Tavistock in September 1941, Ivan enjoyed the thrill of flying from an early age having won a 'Flying Scholarship' whilst a pupil at Plympton Grammar School. He made his first flight in a Tiger Moth on his 17th birthday and, obtaining a Private Pilot's Licence three months later, quickly gained experience by ingeniously giving his chums flights if they paid the costs! It was no surprise, therefore, that shortly before his 19th birthday he joined No. 83 Entry at RAF College Cranwell as a pilot Flight Cadet on the 6th September 1960, initially flying the Jet Provost,

Towards the end of the course he suffered a serious back injury which determined his future flying career. Deemed unfit for flying in aircraft which depended upon ejector seats for rapid evacuation this virtually eliminated the fast jet scene. There were, nevertheless, a number of other options and after completing his advanced flying training he was posted to Coastal Command and joined No.201 Squadron in December 1964. Initially at RAF St. Mawgan, but later moving to Kinloss in Scotland, he flew the Shackleton Mk3. However, in the spring of 1966 territorial disputes arose between Malaysia and Indonesia which led to confrontation, particularly in Borneo, and Ivan was part of a RAF detachment sent to the area. Initially based at Changi, Singapore, but later at Labuan in Borneo, their area of operations ranged over the Sumatran Straits and the South China Sea.

Flying by night, their main task was searching for gun-runners and also maintaining anti- piracy patrols.

Above: The Shackleton, an ideal long range surveillance aircraft

The dangers of long patrols over dangerous oceans cannot be over-emphasised and, now back in the U.K, Ivan relates one incident which occurred on his last flight in this type of aircraft when they had been tasked with a search for a missing trawler. He said:

"We had spent 15 hours searching for and eventually finding a 'perfectly content' fishing trawler some 500 miles out in the Atlantic when our No.3 engine dramatically failed and caught fire. The weather at the time was atrocious with storm force winds and 60ft seas. Turning for home it was apparent that the contra-rotating propellers of that engine would not feather and continued to windmill causing substantial drag on one side. The fire was eventually extinguished but we needed more and more power on the remaining engines to keep flying. It was now getting critical. The navigator calculated that we would not reach land for another four hours and the engineer saying we only had fuel for three! Our initial 'PAN' call was immediately updated to a full 'MAYDAY' and we started to jettison everything possible into the sea to reduce weight. By now we had an escort of two other Shackletons, one on each wing, and, beating all odds, we made a safe landing. Our fuel gauges were showing empty and a subsequent dipping of the tanks showed we only had four minutes of fuel left! A subsequent

investigation revealed a complete failure of the engine reduction gearing which had welded itself in the heat of the fire and then disintegrated. After landing I went to change out of my flying kit and found an envelope on my locker ... it was a notice I was being posted!"

Ivan's new posting was as Flight Commander at the Aircrew Officer Training School at RAF South Cerney. Whilst an enjoyable tour, he was delighted when it ended and he was posted to RAF Ternhill to convert onto helicopters. It was the beginning of an eventful career and one which brought him back nearer to home in the West Country for in early 1970 he was posted to 'A' Flight, No.22 Squadron, based at RAF Chivenor in North Devon. Shortly after his arrival he became the Flight Commander and it was, he says, *"without doubt the best tour of my career"*. He describes the flying at Chivenor as: *"real, very challenging, always different and immensely satisfying, resulting in many dramatic incidents, close shaves and, above all, the freedom to operate at one's own discretion without restrictive rules and regulations."* Actually Ivan's view was not exactly correct for, due to the basic characteristics of Chivenor's Whirlwind Mk10s, whilst there were no restrictions on day flights if deployed at night they were not allowed to carry out a full rescue. But, as Ivan once said, this was an order which had been subject to interpretation many times in the past It was also one which confronted him in November 1970.

He said, *"It was a very nasty night and I was called to rescue a fallen climber on Berry Head in South Devon. He was seriously injured and lying on a ledge some 15 feet above a very rough sea with gale force winds blowing onto the cliff face. Cliff rescue teams had been trying to rescue him for four hours during the afternoon and had been holding us in reserve in case they failed. Although on arrival we did manage to complete a very difficult rescue, in doing so I had to request that the Berry Head lighthouse be turned off for a brief period as it was blinding me. Big mistake! On recovering the climber into the helicopter from a hover less than three feet from the cliff face (as assessed by the coastguards) his pulse began to fail and, although the winchman worked frantically to resuscitate him, we realised professional medical assistance was required immediately. At this point all radio contact was lost and, unable to arrange a night landing site, we decided to make a direct approach and landing on Paignton promenade which was directly in front of us and all lit up with a telephone next to the road. With traffic coming to a halt left, right and centre, we touched down next to the telephone box - my navigator dialled '999' and within three minutes an ambulance arrived much to our relief as the climbers pulse had ceased but had been restarted by the winchman during our short flight."*

What happened next is worthy of note for apparently Ivan had broken every rule in the book by effecting a full rescue at night with the Whirlwind, causing an 'international incident' by having Berry Head light turned off and landing in an unauthorised place. Needless to say the next day it was headlines in the Press. However the RAF hierarchy was not pleased and a summary of evidence was to be prepared with a view to his Court Martial. Fortunately common sense prevailed and for their brilliant airmanship Ivan, and his winchman, were both awarded the Queen's Commendation for Valuable Service in the Air. One good thing did come out of this episode, the Orders were changed to allow all rescues, both day and night, to be carried out at the Captain's discretion.

However, controversy seemed to follow Ivan when he was involved in another even more toe-curling incident whilst at Chivenor on a misty and particularly busy day in August 1971. Ivan and his crew had already completed three rescues and spent five hours flying in salt laden air when they were called to rescue a seriously injured climber who had fallen down cliffs on Lundy Island. This was completed successfully and they set out to convey the casualty and his wife back the 17 miles to the mainland.

What happened next is described in Ivan's own words:

"We were flying in mist at 100 feet and 90 knots when I began to sense that all was not well. We were losing power and, within seconds, there was a loud bang followed by a rush of hot air into the cockpit and the illumination of the engine's fire warning system. With only a single engine - that was it! I was committed to a ditching which took place seven seconds later. The helicopter rolled over, the nose went down rapidly and within 20 seconds the whole thing sank, taking my winchman with it. In that time, between us we had managed to extract the casualty and his 'non-swimmer' wife, but the winchman's escape had been blocked by the empty stretcher. However, a few moments later the winchman burst through the surface like an orange Polaris missile! It was a very happy moment, for we had all survived and were soon rescued by our second helicopter from Chivenor".

Three weeks later the wrecked helicopter was retrieved from the depths but with no apparent technical fault the subsequent Board of Enquiry found Ivan was culpably negligent. Fortunately these findings were dismissed by the C in C Strike Command whose foresight was later reinforced when Rolls Royce confirmed the engine had stalled following excessive salt ingestion during that days operations. Some 30 years later the incident was made into a BBC prime-time documentary called 'In Extreme Danger'.

During Ivan's stay at Chivenor he had flown 122 rescue missions during which he had airlifted 88 persons out of danger. With such vast experience the inevitable happened, he was promoted to Squadron Leader and posted to the Central Flying School to take command of the school's instructor training squadron. There were many other career highlights including being a member, and later manager, of the 'Gazelles', the RAF's helicopter display team which performed in front of HM the Queen Mother and at the 1975 Paris Air Show.

Above: Ivan's helicopter being recovered from the waters off Lundy Island following their miraculous escape.

Many other appointments were to follow. These included a tour at the Ministry of Defence and the setting up of a Sea King Training Unit at RNAS Culdrose. Then, with promotion to the rank of Wing Commander, came Command of the RAF Search & Rescue Wing at Finningley which was responsible for units from Cornwall to Scotland and even the Falkland Islands. A posting to the Joint Services Staff College in Canberra, Australia, followed which included tours of the South Pacific Islands. Then, returning to the MoD, he became responsible for the future planning of air-sea rescue operations within the UK. After two further tours and a career spanning over 32 years, he decided to retire and return to his West Country roots.

A member of the East Devon Aircrew Association, today he enjoys retirement with his wife, Judy, in a secluded spot of North Devon not too far from Chivenor.

FROM KHAKI to LIGHT BLUE!

Barrie MASTERS

Born at Clifton, Bristol, in November 1928, Barrie commenced a career in banking on leaving school but, called for National Service in February 1947, decided upon a military career when offered a regular commission in the Army. A period at the Royal Military Academy, Sandhurst, followed after which he was commissioned as a 2nd Lieutenant in the Royal Artillery. He subsequently joined No.29 Field Regiment Royal Artillery and saw service with them in Germany, Cyprus and the Canal Zone as well as in the UK. Now a Lieutenant, in May 1951 he began a tour with No.62 Heavy Anti-Aircraft Regiment based in Lincoln but after two years began to consider a change of uniform from Army khaki to Royal Air Force light blue. In September 1953 he resigned his commission.

With the necessary preliminaries completed, in May 1954 he attended the RAF Aircrew Selection Centre at Hornchurch where he was graded suitable for training as a pilot or navigator and chose the former. As an Acting Pilot Officer he undertook his Initial Training at RAF Kirton-in-Lindsey, Lincolnshire, before leaving for Canada in style aboard a luxury liner in the November to commence his flying training. This was undertaken at RCAF Moose Jaw where the aircraft flown was the Harvard and later at RCAF Gimli for advanced flying on the T33 jet trainer, known by the RCAF as the Silver Star.   On successfully completing his training he was awarded his pilot's brevet, having been was promoted to Flying Officer in the August.

Most RAF pilots who trained overseas were required to undertake an acclimatisation course on return to the UK. Barrie undertook his course at RAF Swinderby, Lincolnshire, where the aircraft flown was the Vampire T11, a two-seat trainer version, and the single seat Vampire Mk.5.

Above: The RCAF T-33 Silver Star.
Flown by Barrie at Moose Jaw, it had a top speed of approx. 600 mph.

With acclimatisation completed, Barrie's next posting was to the Operational Conversion Unit at RAF Chivenor where he flew the Hunter in preparation for joining his first operational squadron. This came in August 1956 when he was posted to Germany to join No. 71 (Eagle) Squadron at RAF Bruggen which was equipped with the Hunter Mk4. Their role as a day fighter squadron was to keep a watching brief for intruders from behind the Iron Curtain during a time of great tension. However in May the following year the squadron was disbanded and Barrie returned to the UK to spend a year on non-flying duties.

He was recalled to flying in August 1957 when, after a conversion course on the 4-engine Hastings transport aircraft, he joined No.24 (Commonwealth) Squadron at RAF Colerne. His duties were those as 2nd pilot and co-pilot and he remained with the squadron for four years during which time he was promoted to Flight Lieutenant. It was a period which saw him flying to many interesting locations such as Australia and Honolulu but perhaps the one he remembers best was a 3 month detachment to Xmas Island at the time of the nuclear tests. Asked for his recollections he said:

"Our actual role was to fly in supplies for the troops, mainly food as nothing

grew there. At the time of the blast we were sitting on the airfield with our backs to the blast. We also had our hands over our eyes although, despite this, we could still see the flash through them. Then, about 10 seconds later, we felt a warm blast, like an oven door being opened behind us."

Above: The Handley Page Hastings long-range transport aircraft.

On leaving the Squadron in July 1961 he was posted to RAF Dishforth to qualify as a Hastings Captain following which he was posted overseas again, this time to join No.70 Squadron which was based at RAF Nicosia in Cyprus and, once again, with his Hastings he travelled to many destinations, carrying both troops and freight. When his three year tour ended in November 1964 he returned to the UK and the following month arrived at the A & AEE Boscombe Down, officially the Aircraft and Armament Experimental Establishment but often referred to as the Test Pilots School. It was another three year tour during which he flew a variety of transport and communications aircraft, including the Hastings, Valetta, Bristol Freighter, Devon and a legacy from pre-war and WWII, the Avro Anson.

The end of this tour saw Barrie undertaking a variety of ground posts until a return to flying came in March 1971 when he undertook a refresher course at RAF Manby on the Varsity. This completed, he returned to Boscombe Down for another 3 year tour in the May. The aircraft flown were much as before with the addition of the Pembroke and Basset.

On leaving Boscombe Down for the second time, once again a number of ground positions ensued over the next five years, many of them as an instructor on flight simulators for the Phantom and Jaguar in locations ranging from Coningsby and Lossiemouth in the UK to a return visit to Bruggen in Germany.

Returning from Germany in May 1979, Barrie was posted to join No.207 Squadron based at RAF Northolt as a communications and VIP pilot. Flying the twin-engine Devon, he was also at this time qualified to support the Battle of Britain Memorial Flight.

The Basset   The Devon.

Barrie's tour at Northolt ended in November 1983 when, having reached the age of 55, he retired from the RAF after almost thirty years service. However, that was not the end of his flying. He became a Flight Simulator instructor for Airways Flight Training at Exeter Airport and then in 1986 combined this with membership of the RAFVR No.4 Air Experience Flight. For the next 8 years he gave air experience flights to cadets in the Flight's Chipmunk aircraft until March 1994 when, sadly, having passed the age of 65 he had to retire.

Today he enjoys his retirement in Tiverton and is a member of the Taunton & Tiverton Aircrew Association.

WINDSOCKS CAN BE DANGEROUS!

Peter MAY.

Although born in Monmouthshire at the end of March 1919, Peter was Educated at Huish Grammar School, Taunton, and after leaving started a career in insurance. However his interest in aviation started much earlier in the early 1930's when his friend's brother landed an Avro bi-plane near them whilst training to be an RAF pilot. Then, soon afterwards, Sir Alan Cobham visited Taunton with his 'Flying Circus' and offered Peter and his friend a flight in exchange for taking tickets at the gate to the field where the flying was taking place. Their reward turned out to be one circuit of the field!

In 1937, at the age of 18, Peter applied for a Short Service Commission in the RAF but as re-armament was not yet encouraged he was not accepted but instead joined the Civil Air Guard at Weston-super-Mare where members would be taught to fly for 2s6d an hour. However at the declaration of war Peter and two colleagues immediately made plans to travel to London to appear before an aircrew selection board. His colleagues were accepted for training as a navigator and gunner, respectively, and Peter as a pilot.

He duly arrived at Downing College, Cambridge, for initial training then, in June 1940, to a holding unit at RAF Hemswell, near Lincoln, from where Hampden bombers were making night flights over Germany to drop leaflets. Peter was detailed to man a Lewis gun, one of many around the perimeter, and saw his first enemy action when the airfield was bombed. Later that month he arrived at the EFTS, Carlisle, to start flying training in earnest and, flying the Magister, made his first solo flight on the 26th June 1940.

Two weeks later he had a narrow escape when his engine failed but managed to make a safe landing for which he was commended and later selected as one of only six out of fifty for further training as fighter pilots. This continued at No. 5 SFTS, RAF Sealand where the aircraft flown was the Miles Master. Peter recalls one incident when, in a daring moment, he flew under the Menai Bridge which links Anglesey to the mainland.

Left: The Miles Master.

On the 10th December 1940 Peter was posted to No. 57 Operational Training Unit where he flew the Spitfire Mk I, one of the first to be produced. It was whilst here that he had another lucky escape as he now describes:

"I was flying at 5000 feet over Liverpool when once again I had an engine fail and through the haze the only flat area I could see was the River Mersey. The 2½ ton Spitfire without power has a gliding angle like a brick and I learnt later there was little chance of surviving a water landing. However at the last moment I saw Speke grass aerodrome and, using the emergency bottle to lower the undercarriage, just managed to clear the boundary hedge."

In February 1941, with a total of 150 flying hours, of which just twenty were on Spitfires, Peter was posted to join No. 74 Squadron at Biggin Hill, later moving with them to RAF Manston. This was also in Kent but much nearer to the Channel coast where their operational role was twofold, the escorting of convoys through the Channel and the protection of Air Sea Rescue craft picking up downed aircrew. Although he mentioned being 'jumped' from above by a number of Me 109's whilst at 31,000 feet, he prefers to relate a particular incident occurring a few days later:

"The duration of a Spitfire was about 1¼ hours with 87 gallons of fuel and on the 21st April 1941 we had been patrolling at 25,000 feet for 1½ hours so with a fuel shortage our Squadron Leader decided we should land in formation. I was on the outskirts of the formation and collided with the windsock as a result of which the Spitfire disintegrated and I finished up with concussion and a broken leg. After initial treatment in Margate General Hospital I was to spend the next two months in the aircrew ward at RAF Hospital, Halton."

Left: Peter's wrecked Spitfire after hitting the windsock

Peter's near miss with death made him realise how lucky he had been as he recalled the fate of many of his former colleagues. *"Whilst recuperating I learnt that of the eight of us who were originally posted to either Nos. 74 or 92 Squadrons in February 1941 only two were still alive, Tommy Rigler who had also been injured and myself. Such is the luck of the draw,"* he said.

Finally declared fit in April 1942, Peter's next postings covered a refresher course and a Fighter Gunnery Flight before eventually joining No.1 Squadron at RAF Tangmere to fly Hurricanes. He recalls that their C.O. was a Sqn.Ldr. MacLachlan who had a mechanical left hand to replace his natural one which had been shot off during an air battle over Malta. Their sorties mainly comprised fighter sweeps over the Channel but, in the July, plans were made to convert the squadron into a night fighter one. Peter was sent on a night flying acclimatisation course with 21 hours of flying on the twin-engine Oxford. However the result was not what he expected for, classed 'above average', he was posted to No. 1528 Beam Approach Flight as an instructor. Here he amassed another 700 flying hours and in April 1943 was commissioned.

When in August 1944 the Flight was disbanded Peter was posted to Skeabrae in the Orkney Isles as C.O. of a Communications Flight, comprising a wide variety of aircraft including Martinet, Oxford and Spitfire. Here another 150 hours were added to his log book. However, he was keen to join a transport squadron to obtain experience on the Dakota with a view to joining Imperial Airways post war and here the saying *'it's not what you know but who you know'* was to play a part. By chance, Peter had a distant relative who was a WAAF officer working in the postings department at the Air Ministry. With some forethought he flew to London and took her out to dinner. The journey was successful for he says, *"When I returned to Skaebrae, surprise, surprise, I was told I was being posted to Weston Zoyland to await a vacancy for training on Dakotas. It was only ten miles from home"!*

From February 1945 he flew Hurricane night sorties from Weston Zoyland whilst awaiting the promised course on Dakotas. This later came at RAF Crosby on Eden near Carlisle and in May Peter had just completed his first 'solo' flight in a Dakota when news of the German surrender came through.

The course was abandoned and he was posted to No.667 Squadron, Gosport, as Naval Liaison Officer where, flying the new Spitfire Mk.XVI, he helped in the training of naval gunners. However to get South he 'hitched' a lift in a USAAF B-17 being flown from Edinburgh to London. The Captain invited him to take the co-pilots seat but what happened next amazed him as he now describes:

"At the end of the runway, whilst waiting to take-off, he pulled out his cigar case and lit one. I declined his offer of one but I must admit to lighting my very first cigarette whilst flying. Later I asked what he had been doing in Edinburgh and he said they had just flown up to fill the bomb bay with Scotch whisky for a mess party ... some party! "

Peter made his last flight in a Spitfire on October 16th 1945 and left the RAF shortly afterwards with the rank of Flight Lieutenant. He then joined No.10 RFS, RAFVR, based at Exeter Airport but in August 1950, during his two weeks annual training he was seconded to Transport Command at RAF Bassingbourne as 2nd pilot on the 4-engine York transport aircraft. He says it was an interesting fortnight, flying spare engines for aircraft based at RAF airfields in Egypt and Iraq. The following year it was night flying as 2nd pilot on an Anson taking mail from Croydon to the Continent via Guernsey, Paris and Brussels. However, when not on detachment, he flew from Exeter where, in 1951, Chipmunks replaced the aged Tiger Moths. Whilst here he recalls how on the 17th September 1952 they searched for a naval Firefly which had ditched in the Channel. The crew were found in a dinghy 35 miles off Start Point and saved by the local lifeboat with their help. He made his last RAFVR flight on April 19th 1953 but now the holder of a Private Pilots Licence he continued to enjoy flying as a member of the Exeter Flying Club.

On leaving the RAF, Peter entered banking, retiring as a Bank Manager. Today, in his 90's and a member of the Taunton and Tiverton Aircrew Association, he enjoys retirement back where he grew up, in Taunton.

'FROM BOMB MAKING TO BOMB DROPPING!'

Peter MORRIS

Son of a London policeman, and born in the East End in June 1925, Peter has many vivid memories of the London blitz. In May 1941 he lied about his age to join the newly formed Air Training Corps and later, at 17¼ years of age, applied for aircrew. Assessed suitable for pilot, navigator or bomb-aimer training, he was enrolled into the RAFVR on the deferred service list until reaching the age of eighteen. On the 14th June 1943 he was called for duty and his aircrew training began at No.9 ITW at Stratford on Avon. Grading on Tiger Moths followed at Marshal's Airfield, Cambridge, after which he was selected for navigator training. However, it was now mid-1944 and with aircrew losses diminishing replacement was no longer a priority. As a result Peter was initially posted to a 'bomb dump' to assemble fuses in 4000lb bombs for Lancaster bombers. A posting to RAF Jurby, Isle of Man, then came for his long awaited navigator course with flying in the Anson. On completion he was awarded his coveted navigator's brevet but by now the war in Europe had ended. Nevertheless, after a period of leave, he was posted to an Operational Training Unit for crew training on the Wellington preparatory to joining 'Tiger Force' for an ultimate onslaught against the Japanese. However, as history records, the American dropping of A-bombs on Hiroshima and Nagasaki brought a swift conclusion to the war and 'Tiger Force' became redundant.

Hostilities over, Peter was posted to RAF Tuddenham, a rudimentary wartime airfield in Suffolk, to join his first squadron, No.90. This operated the Lancaster and had been tasked with photographing the whole of Great Britain for mapping purposes. They also made occasional flights to Germany, flying in formation at low level with up to fifty other aircraft, the objective being to make a show of force during the Nuremberg trials. The return from one such flight left quite an impression as he now recalls:

"We came out of cloud at very low level and were right over the centre of Cologne. I could see the cathedral and the bridges over the Rhine, all of which had been destroyed. There was hardly anything standing apart from the cathedral."

It was now early 1946. Peter signed on for a further three years and just before his 21st birthday undertook an instructors' course at RAF Finningley. Returning to rejoin his squadron in Suffolk early the following year, he moved with them when they re-located to RAF Wyton and re-equipped with Lincolns. However they also downsized from twenty to only eight aircraft as many aircrew had left the service and at one time the squadron had only two navigators which meant Peter was in demand. He made flights to Egypt where, amongst other exercises, they practiced bombing in the Canal Zone, once flying along the course of the Nile at only 100 feet as far as Khartoum in the Sudan. From there they continued to Kenya, again following the Nile at low level and able to see crocodiles in the river. On arrival in Nairobi they performed a 'Battle of Britain' day display, their Lincoln at that time being the largest aircraft ever to land there. At the end of year Peter was on the move again, this time to RAF Conningsby, Lincs., to become an instructor on radar at a Mosquito training unit. It was not a move he relished, mainly because most of the pilots were very inexperienced and of the 24 students who passed through his hands during his six months there, 18 were killed within two years.

He was glad when his detachment ended with a posting to RAF Lindholme, near Doncaster, and a return to flying the Lancaster with more flights to Egypt. However, for one such flight he was detached to Waddington to be a navigator on a flight of ten aircraft aiming to make the first non-stop flight between the base and the Canal Zone. It turned out to be an experience Peter will never forget. A violent storm near Malta saw them blown off course to such an extent they ended up over the Sahara Desert, three hundred miles to the west of their planned landfall at Alexandria. Despite having been fitted with extra tanks their fuel situation was desperate and, on reaching the Canal Zone, they had been airborne for fourteen and a half hours. They were cleared for an immediate landing and when the fuel tanks were dipped, they had less than fifty gallons left, hardly enough to make another circuit! Also an examination showed the storm had stripped all the paint off the leading edges of the wing and the wing itself was covered in dents the size of table-tennis balls. Of the ten aircraft which had left Waddington Peter's was the only one to make it direct.

Still non-commissioned, Peter decided to extend his service to a full 22 years and in due course was posted as an instructor to RAF Swinderby, an Advanced Flying School flying Wellingtons which he described as being so old they were virtually death traps. With relatively inexperienced students, the fatality rate was high, an occurrence which once brought comment from the local coroner. They were replaced when Swinderby was the first to receive the new Vickers Varsity. Ironically it was whilst undertaking a familiarisation flight on the new aircraft that Peter had his only crash which occurred when there was a fault in the aircraft's undercarriage causing it to collapse on landing, luckily without injuring either Peter or its two pilots.

After Swinderby, Peter was posted to Oldenburg, Germany on a ground tour as a 'fighter plotter', and also promoted to Flight Sergeant. He still managed a few flights with an Anson and recalls one mysterious flight to Berlin.

"Before take-off we taxied to the far side of the airfield where we stopped to allow a male passenger into the aircraft. We then took off and, flying through cloud, navigated the narrow corridor through the Russian Sector and, breaking cloud just before our arrival, we could see a large Russian tank training ground. On landing in Berlin we went to a remote part of the airfield where our mysterious passenger alighted and disappeared. To this day we have no idea who he was or what was his mission."

Above: A newly arrived Vickers Varsity at RAF Swinderby in 1953

On completion of his tour Peter returned to the UK and was posted to Coastal Command, ultimately joining No.42 Squadron at RAF St. Eval in Cornwall and was there when they converted from the Lancaster to the Shackleton. Part of their duties involved Colonial Policing when four aircraft were detached to Aden for short tours of three months. Here Peter's crew patrolled the Yemen/Aden border on the lookout for raiding parties. Another role was to drop leaflets warning the population to behave or face the consequences, sometimes with a not too friendly response. In fact, once ordered to drop leaflets on a hostile fort from a height of about 500 feet, their Shackleton with strafed with bullets, some entering the fuselage and two piercing the wing. However retribution was swift and the following day the fort was attacked by paratroops and the SAS, the rebels ousted and the fort blown up. On another occasion Peter's crew was the retribution, dropping 1000lb bombs on hostile tribesmen from the Yemen who were carrying out raids on the Aden side of the border. In between such missions it was flying as usual from St. Eval.

However the middle of 1958 was a defining moment in Peter's career for now the RAF's policy was that all pilots and navigators should be commissioned and he was still a Flight Sergeant. He was told that as an NCO he was no longer be able to fly with an operational squadron but was given the opportunity to train to operate the new Thor intermediate range ballistic missiles. Having accepted the challenge he was sent for training near Tucson in the United States, although it was some time after his return to the UK that the missiles actually arrived, and when they did he found the routine very boring. However he was promoted to Master Navigator and later asked again if he would accept a commission. He did and after a course on the Isle of Man was promoted to Flying Officer.

This meant a return to operational flying and towards the end of 1961 Peter was posted to join No.120 Squadron at Kinloss to be re-united with the Shackleton. Most of his sorties from here involved long flights over the North and Barents Seas keeping surveillance on Russian shipping and, in particular, their naval vessels including submarines. This, of course, was at the height of the Cold War and when a potential enemy was spotted it would be shadowed until any potential danger had passed. This could involve flights of up to twenty hours duration. Also of interest were Russian vessels disguised as fishing boats but in essence bristling with electronic tracking equipment intercepting Allied signals, very much 'tit for tat!' However, Peter did not only operate from the UK and in the summer of 1963 went to South Africa with half of the squadron for exercises with the South African Air Force.

It was during one of these that one of the South African Shackletons went missing only for the wreckage to be later found in a deep ravine with all the crew dead. The following year, now promoted to Flight Lieutenant, Peter became a weapons instructor at the Maritime Operational Training Unit at Kinloss, moving with the unit to St. Mawgan, Cornwall, and the following year to become the Chief Weapons Instructor. It was whilst with the Unit that in May 1967 he went on a sortie to locate Sir Francis Chichester who was then nearing the end of his record-breaking solo round the world non-stop sailing venture. They located him near the Scilly Isles and dropped him a good will message but Peter says he was not impressed by the response. *"He did not attempt to pick it up or give us a wave, he just ignored us,"* he said.

Towards the end of his long career Peter turned down an accompanied tour in Singapore in favour of a shorter one year unaccompanied one but when offered redundancy he accepted it. One of his last flights was a survey of the Torrey Canyon, the ill-fated oil tanker which hit a reef off Cornwall. However he sometimes reflects on what might have been for the aircraft carrying his replacement to Singapore caught fire over sea, resulting in the wing falling off. All the crew were killed except for the Flight Engineer.

On the 1st July 1968 Peter left the RAF to join his wife, Elsie, in a Cornish bungalow they had bought earlier during his career. He retrained as a teacher and was fortunate to obtain a post at the local school. Also a keeper of goats, he ran this section of the Royal Cornwall Show for over a decade. When final retirement came they opted to move to Tiverton to be closer to family and today he maintains his aircrew interests as the Secretary of the Taunton & Tiverton Aircrew Association.

OBITUARY for a QUIET MAN

Arthur John 'Jack' MORSE

This short chapter is different from the others in the book for the reason that, sadly, Arthur John Morse passed away during its compilation. Whilst some of the facts were related by him personally, others have come from relatives and service colleagues. Together, a little has been gleaned of his life as aircrew during WWII when the survival rate for those operating within Bomber Command was rated at 6 weeks. This was his story.

Jack, as he preferred to be known, was born in Newport, Gwent, in June 1923. Educated locally, at the age of eighteen he volunteered for aircrew duties and, enlisting in the RAFVR, joined the service in February 1942. To close family and friends his choice of the RAF seemed an unusual one because he suffered terribly from sea sickness. However, the fact that his father had been a member of the Royal Flying Corps during WWI, and seen service in Greece, no doubt played some part in his decision.

Following assessment in the UK, Jack crossed the Atlantic to Canada where he found himself 'out west' at a private flying school in Neepawa which had been taken over by the RAF. Here he began elementary flying on Tiger Moths before advancing to the Harvard but, like many before him, did not complete the course and was posted to No.3 Bombing & Gunnery School at MacDonald in Manitoba. Here he trained on the ill-fated Fairy Battle, an aircraft designed pre-war as a light bomber and first entered squadron service with the RAF in 1937. However, their performance and defensive capabilities was no match for the Luftwaffe opposition and during the first year of the war they suffered such heavy losses that by the end of 1940 all had been withdrawn from operational service. Now relegated to a training role, approximately 800 hundred were shipped to Canada and it was here that Jack was introduced to the aircraft and, in particular, their single rear facing Vickers 'K' type gun.

Above: The Fairey Battle.

On successful completion of the course Jack returned to the UK to undertake a further stage of training at No.17 Operational Training Unit where crews were equipped for future operations with front-line squadrons. Destined for Bomber Command, Jack also attended No.5 Lancaster Finishing School at Syerston, Lincolnshire, before commencing operations. He was initially posted to No.106 Squadron at RAF Metheringham but later moved to No.97 Squadron at RAF Coningsby. Both formed part of 5 Group Bomber Command and were destined to play a vital role as part of the RAF's Pathfinder Force.

Those who knew Jack would describe him as being a very quiet, modest and unassuming person and not one to say much about his wartime exploits. As a result we can only draw upon snippets of information which have filtered through. For instance, we know that it was the 'toss of a coin' which saw him take on the role of rear gunner in his Lancaster.

It was recognised that the 'Tail End Charlie' was the most dangerous position within the bomber, usually being the first target for any intercepting enemy fighter. Apparently Jack and his good friend both achieved high marks during their gunnery school course so decided to 'toss' for who occupied the rear turret. Jack lost ... so his friend went to the 'mid-upper' position.

Left: A Lancaster in flight illustrating the isolated position of the 'tail end Charlie' from the rest of the crew

Ironically, despite the many dangers Jack was to face it was not the enemy but the cold which came closest to costing him his life.   Flying at high altitude, particularly in winter, meant that crews were operating in sub-zero temperatures and although heating systems were installed these were primitive by today's standards and often failed.   Arguably, the coldest position of all was the rear turret as Jack was to learn to his cost during the return from one particular raid on Germany.   Fortunately a watching brief by one of his crew was to save his life for, not having heard from Jack for some time, he decided to go to the rear and investigate.   It was lucky for Jack that he did for the extreme cold had frozen Jack's oxygen mask and he had collapsed over his guns.   He was dragged from the turret and then his pilot made the brave decision to take the Lancaster down to low level where oxygen was no longer required and Jack could be revived.   As we now know it was a manoeuvre which was to save his life.

Another interesting fact to emerge from Jack's service history is that his aircraft was one of the few in Bomber Command to be crewed entirely by Officers, Jack being commissioned as a Flying Officer. As stated earlier, his second Squadron, No.97, was part of Pathfinder Force and here we are indebted to Wing Commander Ken Cook DFC who had also served with 97 Squadron and remembers Jack from their days at RAF Coningsby when he had returned to the station for his second tour. Ken throws some light on operating within the Pathfinder Force and says, *"Basically our role was to go ahead of the mainstream bomber force and, having located and identified the targets, drop flares to act as markers for the bombers following us. Needless to say flying ahead of the others was not without an element of danger and during 1944 in particular, 97 Squadron was engaged in dropping markers for some of the most heavily defended of Germany cities. These included Berlin, Munich, Essen and Nuremburg."*

When the war in Europe ended, like many other aircrew, Jack stood by to join 'Tiger Force' for the final onslaught against the Japanese. However this was never deployed due to the rapid cessation of hostilities following the dropping of the A-bombs on the Japanese homeland.

Flying Officer 'Jack' Morse finally left the RAF in October 1946 and initially found employment at Harrods, the prestigious London store. Later he was to join Courtaulds, a major textile manufacturing company, before becoming a business consultant and moving close to Exeter University with his wife Alethea whom he married during the war years.

Jack sadly passed away on the 17th January 2011 and at his funeral family and friends were joined by colleagues from the East Devon Aircrew Association.

A HERCULEAN NAVIGATOR!

Joe OLDFIELD

Born in Woking, Surrey, in June 1945, Joe completed his education at Guildford Grammar School but finding his career choice of training to be a solicitor was not providing enough excitement turned his thoughts to flying. Leaving his solicitor's office, in January 1967 he enlisted in the Royal Air Force to commence training as a navigator. It was the beginning of a career which would take him to all parts of the globe and become one of the RAF's most experienced navigators.

Joe's navigator training began at the RAF Air Navigation School, Gaydon, with astro-navigation a major subject and flying in Valetta and Varsity aircraft. The second half of the course was at RAF Stradishall with practical flying in the HS 125 Dominie illustrated below.

On completion of the course, and award of his 'N' brevet, Joe's next move was to the Hercules Operational Conversion Unit, (OCU), at RAF Thorney Island from where, at the end of 1968, he joined No.30 Squadron. Based at RAF Fairford, the Squadron flew the C-130 Hercules and by early 1969 were flying to the limit as Joe now explains:

" Cut backs in our Armed Forces meant military facilities were being withdrawn from our bases 'East of Suez' and I was soon flying what became known as the 'Changi Slip'. Whilst troops were being brought home in aircraft such as the Britannia and VC-10, the Hercules was the RAF's workhorse and we were flying a constant shuttle from Fairford and Lyneham to the Far East, bringing home a wide variety of equipment, stores and vehicles. Spending up to fifty hours a week in the air was not uncommon. "

However, in 1970 the airfield at Fairford was required for trials of the world's first supersonic airliner, Concorde, and as a result the Squadron relocated to RAF Lyneham. The squadron was part of what was known as the JATFOR (Joint Air Transport Force) with a far ranging role and operated world-wide. During his No.30 Squadron tour Joe spent three months in the Caribbean when trouble erupted on the British island colony of Anguilla. Serious rioting associated with an independence movement saw British troops and a contingent of police from London's Metropolitan Force being sent to restore order. Joe and his crew's role was to ferry men and ensure a supply of equipment and other necessities.

Other activities saw Joe operating from Madagascar during the Beira patrol which was the blockade of Southern Rhodesia after it had declared unilateral independence from Britain. Again, their role was to ensure supplies reached our Forces operating in the area. However, it was not always the military which needed supplies and on more than one occasion he participated in humanitarian flights. These were various and included taking aid, mainly tents, to Turkey following a massive earthquake and later flying grain to the starving people of Ethiopia following sustained drought in that country.

Many of his flights conjure up a James Bond image and, surprisingly, this is not far from the truth for he played a part in 'The Living Daylights' which starred Timothy Dalton as 007. In it, following a briefing with 'Q', James Bond is despatched to Gibraltar where he is seen parachuting down to land on 'the Rock'. Actually it was not the star but a stunt double! How do we know, well the navigator of the Hercules from which the jump was made was Joe! In fact the photograph of Joe which appears at the start of his story was taken on that flight.

In November 1972 he returned to No.242 OCU at Thorney Island, only now as an instructor in a specialist role of training crews for long range operations. This meant that, as well as flights to the popular Mediterranean destinations of Malta and Cyprus, much of the training involved cross Atlantic flights to Canada, Bermuda and Washington DC. However, defence cuts saw the closure of an RAF station, this time Thorney Island, and the OCU, together with Joe, was transferred to Lyneham. Between posts Joe headed to the East once more. He had been selected for a survival course in the steamy jungles of Malaya!

In 1978 he commenced his only 'ground tour' of his thirty year career with a posting to HQ Near East Air Force located at Episkopi in Cyprus. Here the role was jointly air sea rescue and Intelligence gathering. The latter involved the deployment of aircraft to keep surveillance on 'unfriendly' vessels using the Mediterranean. Whilst exciting in some respects, Joe says that the most exhilarating part of the tour was driving home from Cyprus with his wife, Anne. They had purchased a Honda car whilst on the island and, on roads which bore little resemblance to what we know today, navigated their way across Greece and through what was then Yugoslavia.

On his return he joined No. 47 Squadron based at Lyneham, the role of which was mainly low-level support flying with paratroops and stores but shortly after his arrival Argentine Forces invaded the Falklands and Britain became involved in a very long-distance war to recover the islands.

Above: A pair of low flying Hercules.

Getting troops to the islands, and supplying them thereafter, became a major exercise and one in which Joe became very actively engaged for two years of his career. Their route to and from the UK would be via Dakar, Senegal, to Ascension, a remote island in the middle of the South Atlantic. From there it was a further 3,600 miles to the Falklands but because of prevailing headwinds in the South Atlantic this final leg of the journey could not be undertaken without re-fuelling in flight. Constantly changing local weather was another problem as Joe now relates:

"On one flight we had been given a weather forecast which transpired to be badly wrong for, after our 3,600 mile flight, we found the airfield at Stanley completely fog bound. We had no alternative but to make a diversion to Montevideo in Uruguay, another four hours flying away. We also had a very

motley passenger list on board which comprised, amongst others, an Admiral and a Forces entertainment party which included two beauty queens, Miss England and Miss Blackpool. We were well looked after and I had a good night's sleep in a first class hotel after 20 hours airborne but the real point was we had strict orders not to fly within two hundred miles of the Argentine. Ironically, when I looked out of my hotel window I had a view across the River Plate and there, on the other side, was the forbidden country. On another occasion our aircraft did not have the necessary refuelling probe, so it was necessary for us to land at a military base at Canoas in Brazil. It caused quite a stir but the Brazilian pilots were very friendly and came to the aircraft with drinks on a tray. They told us that they, too, had little love for the Argentines. That was not quite the end of the story because the British Press were now in the Falklands watching every move and when we arrived in our Hercules without refuelling facilities they asked how we had managed it. We told a little 'white lie' and explained we had experienced an exceptionally strong tail wind!"

However what was to eventually set Joe apart from most navigators was the fact that he was one of a very select few, only five crews in all, destined to work with 'Special Forces' and In 1984 he joined the Special Forces Flight of No.47 (SF) Squadron. Remaining at Lyneham, he now operated with both the SAS based at Hereford and the SBS based at Poole. He will only say that training for desert warfare took place in Jordan, winter operations were in Norway and for the jungle it was Malaya; also much flying was during darkness using night vision goggles.

A two year respite between 1988-90 saw a switch in roles at Lyneham when he joined the Standards Evaluation Unit with a responsibility for checking the efficiency of other navigators. When this ended he became involved in 'Special Duties', a worldwide role which involved many clandestine and sensitive operations which are still 'classified '. In fact he will admit to no more than taking part in the first Gulf War and operating against drug cartels in South America.

Remaining at Lyneham, Joe began the last tour of his career when he joined No.70 Squadron in 1994. However, once again he found himself in a war zone, this time Bosnia. He says, *"Our role was ferrying troops and supplies but also bringing out evacuees. Flying into Sarajevo and Tuzla we frequently encountered small arms fire and the threat of missiles."*

Uniquely, apart from one ground tour, the whole of Joe's thirty years service was spent on one aircraft, the C130 Hercules in which he amassed an almost record breaking 12,000 flying hours. In January 1997 Joe left the 'Fat Albert' world but not aviation.

He became Company Navigator for Channel Express and, later, European Aviation at Bournemouth. During this period he was trained by Boeing in Seattle on B737 and 747 aircraft performance. However in 2005 he became the Company Navigator for 'Europe's Largest Regional Airline' - FlyBe, based in Exeter. It was a role which saw him return to Brazil to evaluate the runway performance of the Embraer 145 and 195 when FlyBe added them to their fleet.

Finally retiring in 2010, Joe and Anne live not far from Exeter airport and he keeps in touch with his RAF days through membership of the East Devon Aircrew Association.

LAUGHTER - SILVERED WINGS

John PASCOE-WATSON   AFC

A native Devonian, born in Exeter in March 1927, John was educated at Exmouth Grammar School. He says his interest in flying started at the age of 3 and he had his first flight at the age of 5 in a De Havilland Rapide from Alan Cobham's Flying Circus which landed near Clyst Honiton. With his grandmother living close to Exeter Airport, it was no surprise that at the age of 14 he joined No.299 (Exmouth) Squadron of the Air Training Corps although, officially, too young to wear the uniform and through the ATC managed to hitch rides in Exeter based aircraft which included the Fairey Fulmar and Boulton Paul Defiant

Two days before D-day, on the 4th June 1944 and still at school, John had reached the earliest legal age for entry into the RAF. He immediately enlisted and was accepted for training as a pilot under the University Air Training Scheme. Initially placed on the 'Deferred Service' list, in April 1945 he was sent for training at Downing College, Cambridge and from there to No.4 EFTS at Brough, near Hull, for basic flying training on Tiger Moths before, in May 1946, progressing to No.19 FTS at the RAF College, Cranwell. Here he was introduced to the North American Harvard which, as a training aircraft, could actually be quite tricky to land.   In December 1946, due to a change in peacetime recruiting policy, John was posted to No.6 FTS at RAF Ternhill where he was awarded his pilot's wings in September 1947.   Four months later, now a Pilot Officer and having spent a short period flying Harvards from RAF Valley on Anglesey, he reported to No.203 AFS at RAF Chivenor and it was here he had his first introduction to the Spitfire.

Like many young pilots stationed close to home the temptation to give the folks a little 'impromptu' display is never far away and here John was no exception as he now relates: *"It was a sunny afternoon and I set off for home at Exmouth where I decided to fly along the seafront upside down. I inverted it near the docks and to my horror my engine quickly stopped, as almost did my heart. I immediately rolled the right way up, looking for somewhere to land. I discarded the grounds of my old Grammar School as being too far so thought about the beach between the Lifeboat Station and Orcombe Point. Fortunately I came to my senses. I tried restarting the engine which, thankfully it did, just before I reached the sand. It was a very chastened young man that flew back to Chivenor having learned a vital lesson that the Merlin at full power does not last long when inverted."*

With all gunnery and battle training completed, John set sail aboard a troopship for the Middle East and the RAF MEHQ at Abu Sueir from where he joined No.208 (Fighter Reconnaissance) Squadron which had recently moved to Nicosia in Cyprus. It was equipped with the Spitfire Mk. XVIII which had a Griffin engine and 5-bladed propeller, and also with side facing cameras for their specific role. His stay in Nicosia was not without incident, particularly on one occasion when instructed to land on the short runway he approached too fast and was unable to stop. Not being able to see what lay ahead he decided to retract the undercarriage with the inevitable result.

In December 1948 the Squadron moved to Egypt, one of their main duties being reconnaissance for the United Nations, of military movements by Israel which in January 1949 had invaded the Gaza Strip in Egypt. Ironically, during such times it is often incidents of a completely different nature which stay in the mind as John now recalls: *"I had to fly back to Nicosia to represent the Squadron at the funeral of one of No.32 Squadron's pilots and for this I had to take with me a large wreath. There is no room in a Spitfire for stowage except in the cockpit which meant I had to fly 200 miles over the sea in a single-engine aircraft with a funeral wreath round my neck. I just hoped it was not an omen!"*

Actually it nearly was for on the 10th August 1950, he suffered a loss of pneumatic pressure which meant an emergency landing on a flooded runway at Khartoum without flaps or brakes, the result being another rather forlorn Spitfire on its nose.

Above: Two of John's Spitfires.
Left: At Nicosia, Cyprus.   Right: At Khartoum, Sudan.

Whilst in Egypt he was posted temporarily as CO of a RAF detachment at Aqaba when King Abdullah decided to pay a visit to the local Arab Legion, using the RAF airfield for his aircraft.   At lunchtime all the local dignitaries were invited to join the King for lunch and, as CO, this included John.

"We were all instructed to sit on the floor," said John, *"in order that the King was at a higher level.   We were also instructed that it was impolite to refuse any item of food, the first course being a dish of boiled sheep's eyes. Not knowing any better I took one and tried to chew it. It was like a rubber ball and I could see the servants were having convulsions. Eventually I got the message and swallowed it - ugh!"*

Flying reconnaissance flights, as he did, gave John cause to reflect when the more recent Gulf Wars occurred, for one of his tasks had been to photograph all Iraq's 'Oil Pipeline' airfields and he wondered whether any of his material had been used in any of the briefings.

Towards the end of his Middle East tour 208 Squadron re-equipped with the Meteor Mk.9. However because of his impending departure John was not allowed to convert which had a significant effect later. On his return to the UK because he was not 'jet qualified' he was overlooked for a posting to a jet fighter squadron but, after a few arguments, found himself posted to the RAF Central Gunnery School to be re-united with the Spitfire. Here his main role was to make simulated attacks on bombers to give their gunners some practical experience. Another aspect of the school, however, was the towing of targets and here they used modified Tempests, another stalwart from WWII. Needless to say it was not long before John had added this one to his log book and then the Balliol, Vampire and Meteor, the latter being the first twin-engine aircraft he had flown. However, it was his prowess with the legendary Spitfire which also saw him a favourite at air shows and displaying at Plymouth in awful weather was one of his performances.

Many incidents occurred, too many to record here, but one aspect deserving comment was a change in towing procedures he introduced when the old canvas drogues were replaced by gliders. Originally these were discarded after each exercise but John devised a method whereby they could be landed relatively safely after use. Costing £25,000 each, John reckons he saved the Air Ministry several million pounds over ensuing years. In fact he was also asked to demonstrate his new procedure to the Canadians. Recognition for his valuable contribution to air-firing training came in January 1953 when he was awarded the Air Force Cross, receiving the award at the Palace from the yet to be crowned H.M. Queen Elizabeth.

Eventually another posting came through which saw him moving to the Operational Training Unit at Stradishall as Flight Commander of the Fighter Recce training flight. It was reminiscent of his earlier days in the Middle East except now instead of the Spitfire he was flying Meteor Mk.9s. One of his flights was to take him to Scotland where, running rather short of fuel, he landed at a R.N. air station near Glasgow where they wanted to charge him 1s 6d per gallon for 500 gallons. In flying clothing and without money he decided to take off again and fly the 40 miles to Turnhouse airport near Edinburgh, an airfield also used by Ferranti. Here they refuelled him for free but, more importantly, he met up with a former colleague who was now chief test pilot for the company. It was a re-union which was to have great significance later.

There was a continuing demand for his display abilities which was to see him making a number of return flights to Germany but when, later, his Station Commander asked why he had not applied for a permanent commission John replied that he had become fed up with being turned down on at least three previous occasions. He was then told that all his senior officers thought highly of him. However in front of a Board of three strangers John admits that his attitude of *'what you see is what you get'* probably did him no favours.

Eventually decision time came in November 1954 when the C in C of Fighter Command, Sir Dermot Boyle, sent for him and told him frankly that it was extremely unlikely he would ever be awarded a permanent commission and asked if he would like to extend his short service one. Recalling his visit to Scotland, and his former colleague in Ferranti, he replied that he had no wish to become the RAF's most senior Flight Lieutenant and had been offered a post as a test pilot with Ferranti. He was advised to take it! On the 26th January 1955 John ended his RAF career after 10½ years service during which he had displayed two distinct sides to his character. On the one

183

he had been a maverick, a calculated risk taker and sometimes a thorn in the side of authority whilst on the other he had been a competent pilot.

A new career with Ferranti now opened at a time when technology was breaking new ground and, in the era of jet powered flight, aircraft were requiring ever more sophisticated equipment. Militarily this meant state of the art weaponry, particularly gyro gun sights and radar, a field in which Ferranti was a world leader. To aid research prototype equipment was installed in various types of military aircraft to be tested by Ferranti pilots. This was John's new and fascinating role and for the next decade he flew a wide range of aircraft, including the Hunter, Canberra and Buccaneer. By the time he was 'promoted' to occupy a Ferranti desk he had 26 different types of aircraft recorded in his log book. Even then he continued flying as an RAFVR pilot giving air cadets experience in a Chipmunk.

Ferranti's Buccaneer.

Today, a widower, he has returned to his roots and lives in a cliff-top home at Exmouth where he keeps a supercharged SAAB for company. He is also a member of the East Devon Aircrew Association and last, but not least, has turned author. His book, 'Laughter - Silvered Wings ' is a delightful and humorous read of some 270 pages of aeronautical incidents which made condensing it into these six pages such a difficult task.

FATAL CRASH SURVIVOR

Glyn ROBERTS

Glyn, who was born in the West Wales mining village of Penygroes at the end of May 1920, was educated at the local Amman Valley Grammar School. A fluent Welsh speaker, on leaving school he commenced a career with the Civil Service and a post in Customs & Excise which saw him moving to London to work with their dockland unit. However his new career was interrupted when in August 1940 he was mobilised and attended RAF Innsworth to enlist in the Royal Air Force. After his brief initial training he was selected for training as an engine fitter which he undertook at RAF Cosford before his first squadron posting. This was initially to No.101 Squadron based at West Raynham, Norfolk, and later in Scotland where he worked on the Boulton Paul Defiant.

It was 1942 when Glyn had the opportunity to volunteer as aircrew and leapt at the chance, commencing training as a navigator the same year at Dumfries. On successful completion of the course he was commissioned and posted to No.12 OTU at RAF Chipping Warden to finalise training on the twin engine Wellington bomber. This was to be followed by a further posting to an OCU for conversion onto the larger 4-engine Lancaster and joining his new crew and first operational squadron. Sadly the future did not work out as planned as Glyn explains in his own words:

"My apprenticeship as a Navigator came to a jarring halt on the 23rd June 1943 when I was injured in a night-time crash landing. Our crew was engaged on our last OTU exercise in a Wellington before converting to Lancasters. One engine failed at about 8000 feet and whilst returning to make an emergency landing on one engine the other engine suddenly gave trouble. With such a loss of power the aircraft became very difficult to control and we were soon down to around 800 feet. Now too low to bale out, our Canadian pilot found an open stretch of the Yorkshire Moors near Skipton on which to undertake a crash landing. He did a wonderful job but unfortunately before coming to a halt we hit a boulder wrecking the front of the aircraft and sadly killing both him and our wireless operator. I was bracing myself mid-fuselage in a 'crash' position but, nevertheless, was injured whilst the bomb aimer, a Canadian, and the gunner, an Aussie, who had been at the back of the aircraft, just walked out."

Above: A Wellington bomber, similar to that in which Glyn crashed.

Engine failures such as that experienced by Glyn's aircraft were not altogether uncommon. A shortage of training aircraft meant that many of the aircraft designated for training purposes were reaching the end of both airframe and engine life and had been withdrawn from operational flying. Indeed subsequently Glyn found that their aircraft was one which had been 'operationally retired'. However with the pressing need for trained aircrew there was little alternative but to keep the aircraft flying as long as possible.

It does however emphasise the fact that flying training was not without its dangers. With both his pilot and wireless operator killed when the Wellington impacted the ground, Glyn was indeed fortunate to survive. His injuries were severe for he had not only fractured his spine but also badly fractured his leg. However, although the spinal injury was very complicated to stabilise, the RAF surgeons did a wonderful job and he was eventually cleared to return to flying ... with one very important proviso as Glyn explained:

I had to avoid parachute landings," he said. *" Had I been posted to a Lancaster bomber squadron as originally intended, and been operationally deployed on raids over Germany, there was always a real possibility that on one of the 'ops' I would have to bale out. Any sudden impact with the ground and my spine was likely to fracture again. It was a risk the RAF did not wish to take so the result was that I was transferred to a Transport Squadron."*

However by the time Glyn's spinal injuries healed sufficiently for any return to flying, it was late 1944 and the post D-day advance across Europe was well under way. In the UK, No.242 Squadron, which was originally a Canadian fighter squadron, was being brought back into service at RAF Stoney Cross as a reserve for No.46 Squadron engaged in Air Transport duties. Glyn was posted to join them as a navigator and ironically had his wish to crew a four-engine bomber. Not the Lancaster, as was the original intention, but the equally large Stirling, an aircraft which never reached its potential as a front line bomber. The Stirling's limitations saw it withdrawn from front line service as the Lancaster reached the squadrons following which it was used for secondary roles such as mine-laying, towing gliders and carrying freight. It was this latter role that Glyn became engaged in when he found himself navigating the routes to North Africa, the Middle East and India. He described his squadron as a 'maid of all work' but had reservations about the use of the Stirling as a transport aircraft, saying: *"It was designed as a bomber when, of course, its deadly cargo was carried in bomb bays which were completely unsuitable for normal cargo. Space within the fuselage itself was extremely limited and the difficult access presented many problems for those tasked with its loading."*

Asked to describe their main cargo he replied, *"Well we flew a lot of meteorological equipment out to the Far East and to India in particular. This was to assist our aircraft with their night flying operations. I also understand that much of the equipment we took out was transferred onto Dakotas which then flew it 'over the hump' into China. What was particularly frustrating was that after a long flight to India more often than not we had nothing to bring back."*

Above: The Short Stirling.

One particular flight Glyn recalls came in 1945 just after the war in Europe ended. It was July and the first General Election to be held in Britain since the war was being held. Voting facilities were provided where possible for British troops serving overseas and the ballot boxes for those in India and with the 14th Army were assembled in India for return to the UK. Glyn's crew was one of those scheduled for this task and he recalls how every time they landed the boxes were immediately placed under armed guard.

As the war ended No.242 Squadron re-located to RAF Merryfield in Somerset and also re-equipped with the York which, although drawing much of its origins from the Lancaster, was conceived as a long-range transport aircraft. Between 1945 and 1946 Glyn navigated flights to India and, recalling his time with the newly introduced York, says that as well as continuing to carry out equipment, and often returning empty, occasionally their flight undertook a more significant role. Although not specifically equipped, their aircraft were occasionally tasked to ferry recently liberated troops from the Japanese POW Camps. In particular these were troops requiring urgent medical treatment.

The Avro York

Demobilised in March 1946, Glyn's war was not entirely without romance for in 1944 he met Betty who was then a teacher in Birmingham. It was a union destined to last as both were from West Wales and later discovered they had been delivered by the same midwife. Post war, he returned to the Civil Service and served in various parts of the country before finally retiring from a senior position in the Department of Health & Social Security.

A member of the Aircrew Association, he and Betty moved to Exmouth in 2008 to be closer to their family, one son now being a consultant at the Royal Devon & Exeter Hospital and the other a Professor at the University of Plymouth. And, "also *to enjoy a game of bowls,* " he said.

LIFE AS A NATIONAL SERVICE FLIGHT ENGINEER

Anthony ROBINS

Tony, as he prefers to be called, was born in Yeovil in July 1932. Educated at Kings College, Taunton, he entered the family's grocery business on leaving school until like all 18-year olds of that era he was called for National Service. His interview and medical were conducted in Exeter when, having been a member of both the ATC and OTC at school, he expressed a preference for the RAF and was given the opportunity to volunteer for aircrew. His actual call-up came in November 1950 and in the days which followed he found himself at RAF Hornchurch for a more intensive aircrew medical and a wide range of aptitude tests following which he was told he would be trained as a Flight Engineer. It was, he says, a position he hardly expected as he had absolutely no engineering experience, only seven 'school certs'.

Training in earnest started at the beginning of the New Year when he reported to RAF St. Athan in South Wales to join No.11 National Service Aircrew Course at No.4 School of Technical Training. It was to be home for the next five months, during which time they were known as 'Cadet Engineers.' Apart from some drill, training covered a wide spectrum of subjects including the theory of aerodynamics and everything there was to know about the Lincoln bomber, a 4-engine derivative of the famous WWII

Lancaster. Tony recalls making three flights in a Lincoln Mk.2 during the course, including two to Germany and which he says, "were *very cold, noisy and uncomfortable.*"

Successfully completing the course on the 25th June 1951 he became a 'temporary flight engineer' and after a short period of home leave reported to RAF Hemswell to await a vacancy at RAF Scampton, home of No.230 Operational Conversion Unit (OCU). Here crews were formed and Tony recalls he had luck with him when he says:

"One of the pilots, whose crew I nearly joined, was later killed when his aircraft crashed and all his crew died with him. Although technically at peace, deaths amongst aircrew were not uncommon. A Jewish lad who slept in the next bed to me, whom we called Moses, was killed with all his crew when they ploughed into the ground on landing. I recall he had a better mattress than me so I swapped them over! Later, the navigator in our crew, a Pole who flew during the war, was killed in a Canberra.

On successful completion of OCU he was promoted to Sergeant and awarded his coveted Flight Engineer brevet. He had been in the RAF less than eight months and his new role was to help the pilot at all times. This included making pre-flight checks of the aircraft, handling the throttles, lowering the undercarriage and flaps, keeping an eye on all the dials and also keeping watch to the starboard side of the aircraft. In addition he kept a log of all pressures, temperatures, fuel and synchronisation of the engines. In fact much the same as a 2nd pilot would do in many aircraft today. Many Flight Engineers would also take the controls to give the pilot a rest but never for take-offs or landings except in an absolute emergency such as the pilot being killed or seriously wounded.

On the 1st November 1951 he was posted to RAF Binbrook to join No.617

Squadron (Dam Busters), Bomber Command, a front line operational squadron. Flying was quite eventful at times and Tony recalls that on one occasion his young pilot thought he would use emergency boost for take-off, a procedure not recommended and which on this occasion resulted with an outbreak of fire in their no.2 engine at a critical moment. In trying to land they came very close to crashing into trees but recovered and eventually the fire extinguishers did their job. However, they were still too heavily laden with fuel to land safely so flew around to burn it off and also to lighten the load they dropped their practice bomb over the Wash and Tony jettisoned their boxes of 'window', metallic foil strips used for radar jamming. Needless to say, the Squadron Commander was not pleased with our pilot.

On another occasion they had a 'near miss' on landing as Tony explains:
"One morning it was still dark and after a long flight coming into land we could see the sodium runway lights quite plainly but as we crossed the threshold to the runway at over 100 mph we hit a fog bank, a complete white-out and could not see a thing. We hit the runway very heavily with the undercarriage oleo legs nearly going through the wing and the aircraft bounced about twenty feet into the air. The skipper shouted 'overshoot' and I banged the throttles right forward and we shot out of the fog, wheels up, flaps in and going around again. The control tower suggested we divert to RAF Valley in North Wales, about 1½ hours flying away but we were all tired and knackered. We'd already been airborne for seven hours at night with the aircraft's four Merlin engines belting in our ears, vibration and on neat oxygen all the time so we said we'd rather crash than go to Valley. The skipper suggested we had another go. As we came in the skipper said, "Engineer, when I say 'cut' cut everything right back and hold it there. Be prepared to turn everything off". We hit the runway heavily again but eventually bounced to a stop. I think it's called a controlled crash landing."

The following day Tony and his crew did an Air Sea Rescue search over the

North Sea for a downed American Sabre jet, finding some floating pieces of wreckage and directing a life boat to the scene.

In January 1952, No. 617 Squadron converted from the Lincoln to the new Canberra bomber, a twin engine jet without the need for a Flight Engineer so for a while Tony became redundant and relegated to odd jobs in the Control Room. However, in the March another posting came through, this time to RAF Waddington to join No.100 Squadron. For the next two months he flew with a couple of Polish pilots of whom he had his own thoughts as he now relates: *"They were crazy, they had been through the war but now had no home or family and could not go back to Poland. It seemed they were not bothered whether they lived or died. But, that said, they were excellent pilots."*

However on the 19th May 1952 Tony crewed up with a Flying Officer Des Delaney and a week later departed for Shallufa in the Egyptian Canal Zone to participate in 'Operation Sun Ray'. Their route took them over Paris at 10,000 feet then to Corsica, Sardinia, Malta and Libya before their final destination. He also recalls that whilst at Shallufa they were called to take part in an immediate search for a very high rank officer, Air Vice Marshal Atcherley, who had gone missing whilst flying a Vampire across the Mediterranean to Cyprus. He was never found.

Tony had many experiences during his stay in Egypt including some tense moments, especially when King Farouk abdicated in July 1952. There was much unease in the country and RAF crews were put on full alert. He returned home to RAF Waddington on August 16th, the flight lasting just short of 13 hours including a night in Libya. Tony says that on the flight home their Lincoln, RE340, was on its last legs with oil pressure dropping on all engines. In fact no.3 engine went into the red just as they reached base and I was about to shut it down. We were glad to get back

The Lincoln

Tony's final months at Waddington were spent engaged on practice bombing on ranges as diverse as Salisbury Plain, the Wash and on the German North Sea island of Heligoland, with many flights carried out at night. However, by now his two years as a National Serviceman was drawing to a close and he made his last flight on 4th November 1952. He had over 330 flying hours, flown in 39 different Lincolns and served on 7 RAF stations, excluding short attachments such as Aldergrove. His pay had been £6 a week plus £1 flying pay. Now succinctly summing up his flying experience he says, *"It was 80% boring, 10% interesting, 9% exciting and 1% pure terror with a dash of fear."*

Returning to civilian life he rejoined the family business and married his sweetheart, Audrey. Today, in retirement, he is a life member of the RAFA Association, a member of the Aircrew Association, enjoys reading and writing and is the author of a book entitled 'Unknown Dorset at War'.

"Coming home on a hammer and string"

G. Harry ROSTRON

Born in Warrington, Lancashire, in July 1914, a few weeks before the outbreak of WWI, Harry is a chemistry graduate from Manchester University and pre-war followed a career as an Industrial Chemist. However when WWII was declared this became a reserved occupation and, although eager to enlist, he was unable to do so until late 1941 when the restriction was lifted provided he volunteered for aircrew. It was an opportunity he immediately accepted and after initial training at ITW in Torquay, he underwent a long voyage in the SS. Arundel Castle to South Africa for training as a navigator, firstly at No.45 Air School, Oudtshoorn, and then No.43 Air School, Port Alfred. Practical experience was gained on both the Oxford and Anson. Awarded his navigator brevet, he was commissioned in Cape Town and then began the long sea journey back to the UK.

It was now April 1944 and his first posting was to No.10 AFU at Dumfries, followed by a further month at No.42 OTU at Darley Moor. However, from mid-June other postings came which were to give an indication of his future role in the war. Firstly at Ashbourne he was introduced to the Albemarle, a large twin-engine aircraft specifically used for glider towing. Initial training involved towing the small Hotspur glider before graduating to the much larger Horsa. Then, still flying the Albemarle, he moved to Hampstead Norris.

In early February he moved again, now to Tilstock to be introduced to the giant 4-engine Halifax, quickly followed by a move to Earls Colne to join No.296 Squadron. Here his log book gives an indication of two of the specialist roles undertaken by the squadron, glider towing and dropping supplies to resistance groups. These were carried in large boxes stored in the aircraft's bomb bay and their contents would include radio equipment, small arms and ammunition, as well as numerous other essential items.

In March, 1945, Squadron activity was at its highest. Although unknown to them at the time, they were preparing for the Allies' final push across the Rhine into the heartland of Germany, code named 'Operation Varsity'. Greatly dependent upon airborne forces, all the intensive training of Harry and his crew was soon to be put to the ultimate test. On the 24th March, as part of the airborne armada, Harry and his crew took off for the German heartland in their glider towing Halifax.   He explains what happened next:

"Our ground forces were now advancing into Germany and a major combined operation was planned for a final Rhine crossing ahead of the advancing troops. As part of this operation our Halifax was commissioned to tow a Horsa glider for the 6th Airborne Division.   Reaching our target zone at Wesel, the Horsa pilot cast off and we made a customary turn to port, firstly to release the tow rope and then to return to base. It was then that we sustained a direct hit from enemy anti-aircraft forces causing extensive damage including damage to our elevator controls.   The aircraft was soon awash with oil and hydraulic fluid and we were losing height. Fortunately the situation was undoubtedly saved through the initiative of our Flight Engineer who managed to contrive some sort of splint using his hammer lashed to the elevator control although we were still unable to maintain height.   I calculated that whilst we would not be able to reach base it might be possible to reach an emergency airfield.   There was one at Merville, near Lille in France, so I worked out a course to take us there. Our

*fuel situation was OK and, although losing height, the rate of decent was not too serious and I felt we had a good chance of making the emergency field. There was, however, one problem. It would be imperative that our pilot made a successful landing first time as it would be impossible to go around again and try a second time! In the event we succeeded without any serious injuries which illustrated a wonderful example of crew co-ordination. In fact there was an acknowledgement to our Flight Engineer in one of our national newspapers which ran a heading **"Coming home on a hammer and string."***

Above: (Top) The Albemarle and (Below) The Halifax, both used for glider towing.

The role of women in a battle zone is often overlooked and here Harry was to witness the bravery and fortitude they often displayed as he now explains: *"During wartime operations it was not uncommon for an aircraft to carry an observer or journalist, BBC reporter or an Intelligence Officer. It so happened that on our ill-fated flight we took a volunteer from the Intelligence Section, a WAAF officer, Rosemary Britten. She went through the emergency showing enormous calm and composure throughout, obeying instructions even with the prospect of a crash landing with absolute calm. A wonderful person, she died from MS some years ago but I recall with fond affection the sight of Rosemary Britten, WAAF officer of Britain in Halifax 'D' Dog, rather oil smeared but still composed to the astonishment of the US ground crew who greeted us when we landed."*

From Merville Harry and his crew, together with Rosemary Britten, were transported back to base in a Dakota, courtesy of the US Army Air Force. Medicals followed which once again passed them fit for flying. However before leaving he took a photograph of the huge, gaping hole in their Halifax's fuselage. Sadly, he says, this was loaned out and never returned.

Harry (second left) and his crew

Mention was made earlier of dropping supplies to resistance groups. Of particular interest were two flights recorded in Harry's log book made to the Norwegian resistance in April 1945, one of 9 hours 20 minutes, the other 8 hours 45 minutes. Harry recalls these were to the far North, near Narvik. However, these were not the only flights to Norway. Others were made to

Oslo in early May 1945, one on the 9th being particularly interesting. Together with other aircraft, their task was to convey a contingent of airborne troops to take over Oslo airfield from the German forces which were still in occupation. Harry describes events after landing as *"there was just a little scuffle, but nothing too serious."* Asked to elaborate he replied, *"Well the problem was that some of the German troops did not know the war was over but luckily our boys soon put them straight!"*

When the war in Europe ended Harry, like many other aircrew, was put on readiness for operations in the Far East. However, as history records, the dropping of A-bombs on Nagasaki and Hiroshima quickly brought about a Japanese surrender and 'Tiger Force' was stood down.

However, there was still two important tasks left, the repatriation of recently liberated POW's and the bringing home of troops no longer required at the battlefront. This was a task allotted to, amongst others, No.620 Squadron of which Harry was now a member. Based at Great Dunmow, and still flying the Halifax which was not an ideal aircraft for their allotted task, they were nevertheless deployed to assist Transport Command with the repatriations. The scale of the operation was huge and over the next few months Harry navigated thousands of miles to bring troops home. In fact between August and the end of October 1945 his log book shows he made numerous flights to Italy, Greece, Czechoslovakia, Malta, Sardinia and Palestine.

In 1946, with all his duties completed, Flt.Lt. Harry Rostron left the RAF to return to 'civvy street' and join the Chemical Division of Unilever, the giant Anglo-Dutch consumer company, eventually having a major role within their Industrial Detergent Division based in Rotterdam.

Still extremely active at 97 years of age, he enjoys retirement close to family in Sidmouth and is an active member of the East Devon Aircrew Association.

A Hong Kong based flying KIWI!

Colin M. STAGG

Colin was born in New Zealand on the 25th November 1951. After education at Naenae College he decided to enlist in the RAF directly from New Zealand under the Commonwealth DOMCOL system. Initially completing three months training with the RNZAF in his home country, which included flight grading during which he went solo in only five hours, he arrived in the UK on Good Friday 1973. His first introduction to the RAF came with a month's course for Professionally Qualified and Re-entry Officers at Henlow, followed by a short period at RAF Church Fenton PFS (Primary Flying School) where he was given 25 hours flying on Chipmunks in preparation for his next posting. This was to the BFTS at RAF Linton on Ouse where between August 1973 and June 1974 he undertook training on the Jet Provost, obtaining his pilot's wings at the end of the course.

Above: The Jet Provost Mk.5. Powered by a Rolls Royce Viper 201 jet engine it had a top sped of 440 mph and a service ceiling of 37,000 feet.

In August 1974 Colin was posted to RAF Oakington for multi-engine training but shortly after his arrival the station was closed under the 1974 Defence Review which resulted in him arriving at RAF Thorney Island in November for 20 hours of flying on the twin engine Andover C Mk1 before attending No.242 OCU for conversion onto the Hercules C Mk1. Following completion of OCU, in July 1975 he was posted to No.30 Squadron, at RAF Lyneham, as a co-pilot. Later that year he participated in Berlin Zone Flying which utilised the narrow air corridor through the 'Iron Curtain' to the still divided city. He recalls one journey he made on foot was through 'Checkpoint Charlie' into East Berlin, a city then very much under Soviet dominance. Another eventful moment during his stay with No.30 Squadron came in September 1977 when he was co-pilot of the crew which won the prestigious 'Lord Trophy' which was awarded for a 'Search and Rescue' competition.

In January 1978 he was posted, still as a co-pilot, to No.47 Squadron (Special Forces) also based at Lyneham. The Squadron was divided into two parts, the 'Main Sqn' comprising fifteen crews and 'Special Forces' (47SF) which had five constituted crews under a Sqn.Ldr. Flight Commander. Colin's stay with the squadron saw a detachment to Canada and many low-level training sorties with both the SAS and SBS. He also participated in a number of air shows, providing tactical displays and also with the Falcons, the RAF's parachute display team. Then in May 1978, he was promoted to Captain, returning to No.47 Sqn. as a 'Main Squadron' Captain. During the next three years he became Captain Leader and then Deputy Fight Commander (Ops). This was a period which saw him making flights to Hong Kong and to the Woomera testing site in Australia. There was also extensive tactical low level training and, eventually, operations involving formations of aircraft using an American Position keeping radar called SKI. He says that a major highlight was leading one of these ten aircraft formations on a formation drop of a Para Brigade.

However in May, 1982 he returned to 47 SF. Intensive air-to-air refuelling exercises took place, their necessity soon becoming obvious ... the Falklands War. Colin and his crew were detached from Lyneham to Ascension Island and the following month he and his crew were to make five long return flights to the Fleet to make essential airdrops. He says that the longest of these was 26 hours 5 minutes and that all of his flights required air-to-air refuelling at 4 and 8 hours into the outward flight and then the airdrop of vital supplies to a ship, detached from the Fleet. This normally took over an hour to complete. Then it was the long return flight to Ascension Island of around 12 hours, each flight taking the crew over 7200 miles of hostile South Atlantic waters.

By August 1982 they were able to land at Stanley airport but when it was closed during extension work to facilitate the RAF's Phantom fighters they had to once again return to air-to-air refuelling. This also brought into use another unique activity ... 'snatching', a procedure for retrieving small mail bundles. These were hung on a line between two poles and the Hercules would come in at low level and 'snatch' them with a hook, incidentally a procedure first developed in the 1920's.

Colin spent four years flying with Special Forces, much in intensive training with the Paratroops, SAS and SBS ensuring their readiness for any critical situation which might arise. Although he will not say much about this aspect of his career he does say that with the use of night vision goggles they became proficient at low level flying at night at about 250 feet above ground level. Co-operation with other NATO allies saw him on detachments to Norway, Germany, Portugal, France, USA as well as to Kenya and the Oman. In May 1986 his service with No.47 SF Squadron came to an end with a posting to the RAF Central Flying School at to train as an instructor on the Bulldog. Once again his flying skills came to the fore when he won the 'Bulldog Trophy' for being the most promising new flying instructor.

Above: The Scottish Aviation Bulldog, a replacement for the Chipmunk. It became the primary trainer for University Air Squadrons.

The next 3½ years of Colin's career were to see him in the role of instructor with University Air Squadrons. The first of these was the University of Wales UAS which was based at RAF St. Athan. It was whilst here, in January 1987, that he was promoted to Squadron Leader and given his own command. This was in Northern Ireland where he was posted as the C.O. of the Queens University Air Squadron at Belfast Harbour. He was to remain in Northern Ireland until January 1990 when he returned to the mainland and in particular RAF Abingdon, the home of the London University Air Squadron. However for Colin there was a new challenge to come, a second career in civil aviation.

In May 1990, after 17 years service, he resigned from the RAF. His log book showed a total of 5630 flying hours, the majority on the Hercules. He had also been awarded the South Atlantic Medal for his service in the Falklands and the General Service Medal for service in Northern Ireland during the 'troubled times'.

His first civil appointment came with a small company, Greenclose Aviation at Hurn Airport, Bournemouth, where he instructed on the twin-engine Piper Seneca before moving to Channel Express to fly the Lockheed Electra as a Captain. However, his big move came in January 1993 when he became a 1st Officer with Hong Kong based Cathay Pacific Airlines. Initially he flew the

Lockheed 1011 Tristar which interestingly, was the first airliner equipped with the, then world beating, Rolls Royce RB 211 engines. A versatile aircraft, it is still in use by the RAF today.

However in 1995 Cathay Pacific replaced their Tristars with the Airbus A330, and the following year added the longer range A340 to the fleet. Promoted to Captain in 2002, it is the Airbus A340 which Colin mostly commands today, regularly flying the route between Hong Kong and London Heathrow.

Above left: The Lockheed 1011 Tristar, the aircraft illustrated being adapted by the RAF as a tanker for air-to-air refuelling. On the right is the Airbus 340, an aircraft designated as very long-range large-capacity jetliner. In fact its quoted range is 8000 miles with a full fuel load. Operating at heights of up to 40,000 feet it can carry up to 375 passengers.

Since leaving the RAF Colin has added in excess of 12,500 flying hours to his log books, making a total of over 18,000 hours spent in the air and one to which he continues to add.

Despite his long-distance travels Colin and his wife, Gilly, have made their home in the West Country and he retains his RAF links through active membership of the East Devon Aircrew Association, attending their events whenever his flying schedule allows.

ALSO MENTIONED WITHIN THE BOOK

The Bristol Beaufort - RAF Chivenor 1941

No.616 Squadron Meteor at RAF Culmhead - 1944

.... AND AFTER THAT FINAL LANDING AT THE RUNWAY'S END

The Associations and Organisations that help preserve our aircrew heritage and look after the welfare of our members.

The AIRCREW ASSOCIATION ARCHIVE TRUST
Registered Charity No. 1087354

by
Air Commodore Jack Broughton OBE DL - Chairman of Trustees
and
Air Commodore Graham Pitchfork MBE BA FRAeS - ACA Archivist.

Soon after becoming President of the AirCrew Association in 1997, Air Chief Marshal Sir 'Sandy' Wilson introduced his close friend and colleague, Graham Pitchfork to the ACA Council. For many years Graham had pursued a long held historical interest in military aviation and his recent experiences had convinced him of the need to develop an archive for suitable military aviation material and to record the experiences of military aircrew during wartime and peace. This initiative had been reinforced when he discovered that all the papers and log books of a distinguished senior officer had been destroyed by his family who were unaware of their historical significance and value.

In 1998, the ACA Council voted to develop an Archive and decided to invite Graham Pitchfork to undertake the work of Honorary ACA Archivist. He started to collect suitable material from members including interviews on tape recorders gifted by Messier Dowty. A number of these were loaned to ACA Branches where members recorded interviews for inclusion in the archive. The Council also took steps formally to register the ACA Archive Trust and charitable status was gained in 2001 with a grant of £2000 from the parent body. Initially the Charity Trustees were chaired by Sir Sandy Wilson and included Graham Pitchfork as Archivist and Alan Watkins as the Secretary who wrote the terms of reference for the Trustees and thought up the catchy title of A3T. Ron Mudge was appointed Treasurer and the rest of the Trustees were Nigel Walpole and two non-aircrew members: Tony Edwards and Gerry Tyack owner of the Wellington Museum.

During the development phase there was considerable discussion about where best to place the Archive. A number of museums were considered including the RAF Museums at Hendon or Cosford and Tangmere. At that time Tangmere had just accepted a recently refurbished Hunter aircraft that had been dedicated to the AirCrew Association. However in the end the ACA chose the Yorkshire Air Museum (YAM) at Elvington, near York, as the most suitable location for its archive. Both ACM Sir Michael Knight (a former ACA President) and Graham Pitchfork were already involved with the YAM in a formal capacity. In 2001 the YAM Trustees and the ACA Council representatives signed a formal agreement to proceed with the development of the ACA Archive to be located at Elvington.

The YAM, sited on a former WWII bomber base, was selected as it met the criteria considered essential by the ACA; it owns the real estate on which the museum and its exhibits are located. Further the YAM is a registered museum (No.66) under the National Council for Museums, Archives and Libraries. This ensures that archival material items donated to the YAM are specifically coded and given full protection for permanent conservation for the nation. While responsibility for the conditions for holding and displaying the archive material rests with the YAM, the A3T agreed to support the museum in preserving the A3T artefacts while improving the collection.

Over the years the A3T has made significant artefact, medal and uniform donations to the YAM whilst providing financial support towards the cost of storage, displays and the staff working in the archive section. Furthermore the ACA has urged its members to make full use of the museum and has held a number of its Annual General Meetings on site. In addition a number of ACA Branch Standards have been laid up in the Chapel of Remembrance, a pennant has been donated by the Canadian Government to mark the 60th anniversary of the start of the British Commonwealth Air

Training Plan (BCATP), and a plaque mounted in the Garden of Remembrance to the memory of those who served under the worldwide BCATP.

By 2008 it was clear that to ensure the A3T Archive could easily be accessed by researchers the YAM would need to create a database of all the written work held in the archive. Therefore the A3T Trustees agreed to fund an 18 month project for a curatorial assistant to design and construct software for a database which will be proven before inputting all the items currently held by the YAM. Unfortunately this work was hindered by damage to the archive storage facilities caused by storms that revealed areas of asbestos requiring special removal treatment. Nevertheless work on the database project continued apace and by Spring 2010 some 200 individual memoirs and 60 flying log books together with heaps of library items had been incorporated in a new computer.

The damage to the archive building brought home to the A3T Trustees the need for a modern building to hold the archive at YAM. This requirement was already recognised as a future project by the YAM Trustees but in 2010 their priority was for a second WWII style hangar to house their more vulnerable aircraft collection. The A3T Trustees therefore agreed in June 2010 to launch the A3T Memorial Appeal for funds to build an archive building at the YAM in a style similar to the current buildings on site. It was hoped the appeal would raise sufficient funds that, when added to those remaining to the trust following the dissolution of the parent ACA in 2011, the total would cover the estimated building costs of £100,000. By the Autumn of 2010 appeal donations were being received by the A3T affording an expectation that a permanent memorial to the 33 years of the existence of The Aircrew Association would be erected at the YAM in the near future.

After 2011 the ACA Archive Trust and its associated archive at YAM will remain the sole symbol of the ACA in perpetuity.

In June 2010 a memorial stone was added to the low box hedge in the shape of a three-bladed propeller, the ACA emblem, at the National Memorial Arboretum at Alrewas, Staffs. A service of dedication was conducted by the Revd. Bill Pegg, the ACA Honorary Chaplain, and following the unveiling ceremony the future care of the memorial was officially handed over to the AirCrew Association Archive Trust for safekeeping in perpetuity. A fly-past by Spitfire MK356 from the Battle of Britain Memorial Flight concluded the ceremony.

Above: Air Commodore Jack Broughton accepting responsibility for the future upkeep of the memorial on behalf of the AirCrew Association Archive Trust from Air Commodore Des Richard, the Association's Chairman whilst the Revd. Bill Pegg looks on.

The ACA Memorial at the National Memorial Arboretum

The inscription on the stone reads:

"The AirCrew Association was founded on the 8th September 1977 to foster comradeship amongst aircrew who had been awarded a military flying badge. Membership is open to those who are serving or have served as military aircrew in the armed forces of those nations allied to the United Kingdom and Commonwealth. By 2010, over 25,000 military aircrew had joined and in its formative years it attracted members who had served during the Second World War. In recent years the ACA has attracted aircrew from the Cold War era and from those currently serving as military aircrew"

The ROYAL AIR FORCES ASSOCIATION

As its name implies this is an Association for serving and past members of the Royal Air Force with a current membership of around 70,000. Facilities available to members are many and include respite homes, a charitable fund for those in need and a popular magazine with the title 'Air Mail'. The Association is funded by members' subscriptions, bequests and various events as well as operating a profitable commercial and trading side. However for many members its main attractions are the local branches which operate around the country, and indeed overseas, many of which have their own club premises. Within Devon these will be found at Exmouth, Dawlish, Plymouth, Teignmouth and Torbay. As well as providing bar facilities, many provide meals and even, at Teignmouth, accommodation. At local level social events are regularly held so, too, are various excursions of interest to members. Others simply relish the opportunity to compete in a game of darts or snooker.

Although full membership of the Association is restricted to serving or past RAF personnel it is by no means a 'closed shop'. Since its heyday, just after WWII, those eligible for full membership have been steadily declining for hardly a decade has passed without Government spending reviews slashing the size of the armed forces. Today the whole RAF is but a fraction of the size of one Command during the war. The effect is self-evident. There are simply not enough persons coming through the Service to sustain the viability of many clubs without help from other sources. This has resulted in Associate Membership being available to those who support the ideals of the RAFA without actually having served in the RAF.

It is a life-blood which has sustained many clubs, including that at Exmouth. However, today the Exmouth Club also performs another vital function within the town, that of providing facilities for many other Associations which can no longer fund their own accommodation.

The welcoming bar of Exmouth RAFA Club.
The regular meeting venue of the East Devon Aircrew Association

Those resident in the South West interested in obtaining further information concerning the Association are invited to contact the RAFA Area HQ and South Western Office, RAFA House, Chancel Lane, Pinhoe, Exeter, EX4 8JU. Tel: 01392 - 462088.

Alternatively, information can be obtained from The RAFA Central HQ, 117 Loughborough Road, Leicester, LE4 5ND. Tel: 0116 266 5224 or their web site at www.rafa.org.uk

The RAF and ALLIED AIR FORCES MEMORIAL

War is a terrible thing and none more so than for those who have lost loved ones killed in action. Equally important to remember is the ultimate sacrifice made by the many who died protecting our freedom. Here Plymouth Hoe is the site for one of the county's largest war memorials commemorating the loss of seamen from Plymouth based ships. Other large naval memorials will be found at Portsmouth and Chatham.

However, standing not far from its huge neighbour is another military memorial. This is the RAF and Allied Air Forces Memorial, unique for being the only one which acknowledges the sacrifices of all Allied aircrew during WWII. As well as British and Commonwealth airmen it includes the losses from many other countries, including the United States and Russia. All were united in their actions against a common enemy - Nazi Germany.

The monument, erected in 1989, depicts the bronze figure of an 'Unknown Airman', a figure fully kitted in a flying suit and wearing his Mae West life-jacket. In his right hand he is carrying his parachute pack in readiness for the flight ahead. The grey marble column below is enhanced by a black marble inlay listing the many countries whose aircrew are commemorated here together with various tributes to the role they played.

The ashes of the late Air Vice Marshal Don Bennett, CB, CBE, DSO, have since been interred at the base of the plinth, a fitting resting place for a great airman whose foresight led to the formation of the elite 'Pathfinder Force' which spearheaded so many of the Allied air raids on occupied Europe and the Nazi homeland.

It also lists the losses of the three main Air Forces engaged in the conflict:

> 107, 000 Members of the Royal Air Force.
> 84,000 Members of the United States Air Force.
> 43,200 Members of the Soviet Air Force.
> who made the ultimate sacrifice.
> They flew by Day and Night
> and gave their lives to keep forever Bright
> That precious light
> Freedom

From 2011 an annual service of dedication will be held there on the last Saturday in June as part of the wider events commemorating Armed Forces Day. Joining veterans are representatives from foreign Embassies, civic leaders and families and friends of those in whose honour the memorial stands.

Photographed together on Plymouth Hoe at the 2007 service is Lt. Col. Ivan Lebedev, Assistant Air Attaché at the Russian Embassy, London, who laid a wreath on behalf of the Russian people and Joe Williams, President of the East Devon Aircrew Association who did likewise for the ACA.

SOUTH WEST AIRFIELDS HERITAGE TRUST
Registered Charity 1103588.

Following a large public gathering at Dunkeswell Airfield on Monday, 15th June, 1992, to welcome the WW2 veteran B-24 Liberator 'Diamond Lil', the organisers of the event decided to form an interest group to perpetuate the area's WW2 air history and airfield sites and created the Trust as a registered charity. The visit of 'Diamond Lil', which had flown from the United States, is now featured, together with many other locally operated WW2 aircraft, in 'Quest for Freedom', a 35 minute DVD documentary on East Devon's WW2 airfields.

Helped with a generous grant from the Lottery Fund, the Trust organised a Devon Air Day at Dunkeswell Airfield on Sunday 13th August 2006 when, once again, there was a large public gathering to see a host of historic British and American aircraft, plus a solitary Russian, which formed both static and aerial displays.

The Trust operates from one of the wartime Nissen huts along Marcus Road, Dunkeswell, and has organised 'Air Gala' events at the disused Upottery Airfield in 2004, 2008, 2010 and 2011. These included a visit by a WW2 Douglas Dakota C-47 painted in D-day markings and also a display by the US 101st Airborne Re-enactment Group. Complete with vehicles, this re-created the scene at Upottery immediately before the D-day landings. Other activities undertaken by the Trust have included the restoration of a WW2 sentry box outside Moonhayes Farm, Newtown, near Upottery, in 2005, photographs of this appearing in an earlier chapter on RAF Upottery.

Future restoration work planned, as and when funds will permit, include the continued restoration of some of the WW2 Nissen huts at Upottery Airfield which have been used as farm buildings, and also the preservation of the WW2 control tower which, sadly, will need much restoration work. Fortunately, the original runways were well constructed and are still capable of facilitating single and some twin-engine aircraft. Also on a positive note is the fact that its close proximity to Dunkeswell Airfield means that any air traffic can be controlled from there via a local link.

Currently the Trust is endeavouring to raise funds for an Air Memorial at Exeter International Airport, another former WW2 RAF airfield. A local sculptor, Francis Margaret, has been asked to create a suitable statue depicting a WW2 pilot standing looking skywards with arm raised and hand sheltering his eyes from the sun. A low plinth will contain plaques inscribed with details of the Squadrons, and their nationalities, which were stationed at the airfield. At the time of preparing for print, public donations are still being sought towards the target sum of £65000, with a generous donation of £8,000 already having been received from the Polish Air Force Association in memory of the losses suffered by their squadrons whilst based at Exeter during the early years of the war. Exeter Airport has now been added to the Trust's website and details on their activities, events and donations towards the Exeter Air Memorial can all be found on www.southwestairfields.co.uk

The East Devon Aircrew Association is indebted to one of their Associate Members, Group Captain David Chapman-Andrews RAF Retd., an Exmouth resident, for providing the above information. Incidentally, David is also the producer of the DVD 'Quest for Freedom'; the profits from sales will go towards the Exeter Air Memorial fund.

GLOSSARY

AACU	Anti-Aircraft Co-operation Unit
ACRC	Aircrew Reception Centre
AFC	Air Force Cross
AFS	Advanced Flying School
AFU	Advanced Flying Unit
DFC	Distinguished Flying Cross
CO	Commanding Officer
EFTS	Elementary Flying Training School
FOB	Forward Operating Base
FTS	Flying Training School
HCU	Heavy Conversion Unit
HSL	High Speed Launch
ITW	Initial Training Wing
OCU	Operational Conversion Unit
OTU	Operational Training Unit
QFI	Qualified Flying Instructor
RAAF	Royal Australian Air Force
RAFVR	Royal Air Force Volunteer Reserve
RCAF	Royal Canadian Air Force
RNZAF	Royal New Zealand Air Force
RFS	Reserve Flying School
RNAS	Royal Naval Air Station
RTTL	Rescue and Target Towing Launch
SBS	Special Boat Service
Sqd.Ldr.	Squadron Leader
USAAF	United States Army Air Force
WAAF	Women's Auxiliary Air Force